SPECIFICATIONS GRADING

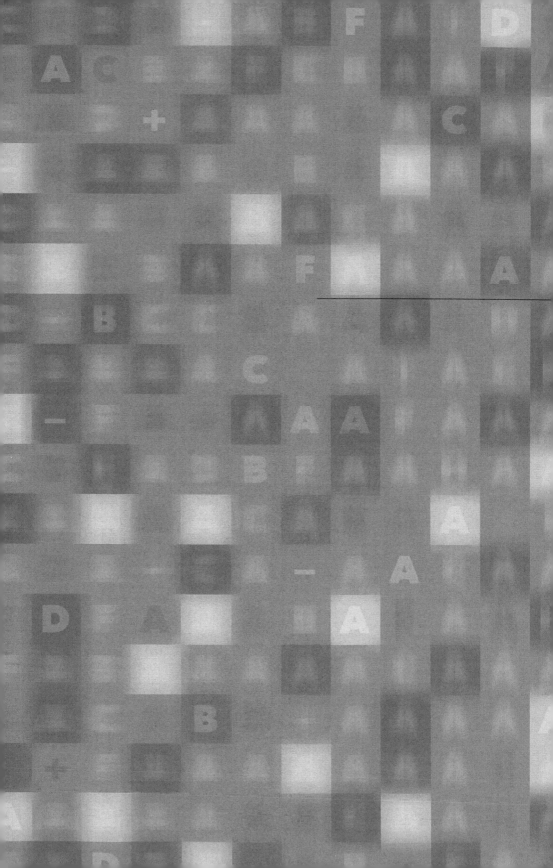

SPECIFICATIONS GRADING

Restoring Rigor, Motivating Students, and Saving Faculty Time

Linda B. Nilson

Foreword by *Claudia J. Stanny*

STERLING, VIRGINIA

Published by Stylus Publishing, LLC
22883 Quicksilver Drive
Sterling, Virginia 20166-2102

Library of Congress Cataloging-in-Publication Data
Nilson, Linda Burzotta.
Specifications grading : restoring rigor, motivating students, and
saving faculty time / Linda B. Nilson.
    pages cm
Includes bibliographical references and index.
ISBN 978-1-62036-241-9 (cloth : alk. paper)
ISBN 978-1-62036-242-6 (pbk. : alk. paper)
ISBN 978-1-62036-243-3 (library networkable e-edition)
ISBN 978-1-62036-244-0 (consumer e-edition)
1. Education, Higher--Standards--United States. 2. Grading and
marking (Students)--United States. I. Title.
LB2368.N55 2015
378.1'6620973--dc23
                                                    2014020284
13-digit ISBN: 978-1-62036-241-9 (cloth)
13-digit ISBN: 978-1-62036-242-6 (paperback)
13-digit ISBN: 978-1-62036-243-3 (library networkable e-edition)
13-digit ISBN: 978-1-62036-244-0 (consumer e-edition)

Printed in the United States of America

All first editions printed on acid-free paper
that meets the American National Standards Institute
Z39-48 Standard.

Bulk Purchases

Quantity discounts are available for use in workshops and for
staff development.
Call 1-800-232-0223

First Edition, 2014

10   9   8   7

In memory of my father

CONTENTS

FOREWORD

Faculty who struggle with the challenges of managing time for grading student work and collecting meaningful assessment data from assignments and projects embedded in their courses will find much to interest them in *Specifications Grading: Restoring Rigor, Motivating Students, and Saving Faculty Time.* Nilson proposes a new approach to rubrics that simplifies the task of grading, maintains standards for consistency and validity of assessments, and aligns grades with specific learning outcomes.

Faculty seldom include the task of grading student work in the list of activities that attract them to teaching and fill them with excitement as they anticipate the beginning of the next academic term. Although evaluating student work and assigning grades is probably the task faculty enjoy least, it is one of the most necessary. At a minimum, institutions required reliable information about the performance of students as a way to hold students accountable for their learning and to provide credible evidence to external stakeholders about the quality of learning associated with the award of course credits and academic degrees. Under the best of circumstances, the feedback instructors provide when they evaluate and grade students' work guides their efforts to improve.

As faculty, we often speak of the rewards we experience when we interact with students, introduce students to a discipline we love, and mentor students as they develop cognitive and disciplinary skills and mature into successful professionals. I have yet to hear a faculty member say, "I am so excited! My students submitted their research papers today and I can't wait to read and grade them!" Instead, we tend to view grading as a difficult, time-consuming, and burdensome process. We fear that students will use our comments and grades on returned work as part of the context for a difficult negotiation over how they might improve their grade (versus their work). Perhaps the only task faculty dread more than facing a tall stack of ungraded papers is the prospect of discussing a grade with an unhappy student. Faculty are no different from other humans; we prefer harmonious relations to conflict. The process of grading is rife with opportunities to create conflict.

What to do? Rubrics solve many challenges posed by grading. Well-constructed rubrics improve our ability to evaluate student work in a fair and consistent manner and can help us complete the task of grading more efficiently. A rubric that clearly describes our expectations can increase the quality of work students submit. If we give our students a copy of the rubric at the time of the assignment, students will fully understand the task and will be more likely to submit work that meets our expectations. The improved quality of work will be enjoyable to read and grading might feel less burdensome. If the rubric describes specific errors and problems we observe in lower-quality student work, we can highlight these descriptions to give students specific diagnostic feedback that explains the decisions we make when we evaluate their work and informs students about how they might improve future work. We can spend less time writing comments when diagnostic feedback appears in the rubric. Moreover, the descriptive language in the rubric helps us make consistent judgments over time. As a result, we can confidently divide a large grading task into a series of shorter blocks and manage the task over multiple days. In contrast, instructors who do not use a rubric often feel compelled to complete the grading task in a single block of time lest they adopt different criteria on different days.

Nilson proposes a solution to the difficult task of writing precise language to describe intermediate categories of quality for rubric elements. Rubrics created for *specifications grading* use a two-level rubric model. Forget the messy task of drafting unambiguous descriptions for intermediate categories for a rubric element. Instead, describe the quality of work expected when a student masters a learning outcome. If submitted work meets that standard, the student merits recognition as competent on that learning outcome. If not, the student must try again to demonstrate his or her competency either by resubmitting the assignment or completing a different assignment aligned with that competency.

Specifications grading addresses a question that has long puzzled faculty: Why aren't the grades earned by students accepted as assessments of student learning? Traditional grades don't work as assessments of student learning outcomes because they merge multiple sources of information about student skill in a single composite score. Factors unrelated to student learning outcomes might contribute to determination of a final grade. For example, instructors may reduce a grade if a student submits a project after the due date or lower a student's class grade if the student accumulates too many unexcused absences from class. Similarly, students might improve a grade by completing "extra credit" assignments or engaging in volunteer activities, although these activities might not align well with a course's learning outcomes. When extraneous variables contribute to how instructors determine a grade or when instructors combine performance assessments across multiple learning outcomes to create a single composite grade, the diagnostic information about student strengths and weaknesses on specific learning outcomes is lost.

Nilson explains how specifications grading corrects the problem created when information about student learning is obscured by traditional processes faculty use to compute a composite grade. However, specifications grading requires more than simply creating a yes/no rubric. Instructors must align assignments and rubrics to specific learning outcomes and articulate which learning outcomes are critical to meeting minimal competency expectations for a given course.

Specifications Grading suggests strategies faculty might employ to design competency-based courses or academic programs that award academic credit based on mastery of student learning outcomes rather than "seat time." Nilson presents models for grading assignments and for combining assignments within a course to document the degree to which students attain competencies expected of all students in the course. The models also enable instructors to document the additional competencies demonstrated by students who exceed these expectations. Nilson describes grading structures that enable faculty to create learning-centered environments that motivate students, document student attainment of intended learning outcomes, and generate a traditional range of grades to recognize and document the achievements of students who exceed learning expectations for the course.

Claudia J. Stanny
Director
Center for University Teaching, Learning, and Assessment
Associate Professor
NSF UWF Faculty ADVANCE Scholar
Department of Psychology
University of West Florida

PREFACE

The intended audiences for this book are all members of higher education who teach, whatever the discipline or rank, as well as those who oversee, train, and advise those who teach. The book offers a new paradigm that I call *specifications grading*, or *specs grading* for short. It gives faculty strategies for developing and grading assignments that reduce time and stress, shift responsibility to students to earn grades rather than "receive" them, reduce antagonism between the evaluator and the evaluated, and increase student receptivity to meaningful feedback, thus facilitating the learning process. It also helps instructors enhance their students' motivation to do well, lower their stress and confusion over academic expectations, strengthen their work ethic, and ensure greater rigor in the educational enterprise. It may even restore some credibility to grades by demonstrating how they can reflect the learning outcomes students achieve. And it is completely within the discretion of the faculty.

Big promises? No denying it. Each promise points to a challenge that typical faculty face. Big promises aim to handle big challenges, and the academy needs some big solutions. Little changes to today's systems will not fix what is ailing higher education. No, big challenges need big changes, *new* systems. This book proposes a new grading system that has solved the problems behind the aforementioned promises for a number of faculty. So this new system is worth broad consideration.

I could elaborate on any of the challenges that specs grading mitigates, but I think that rigor deserves the spotlight for now. I believe it could raise the perceived value and legitimacy of higher education, which has been losing ground and costing the academy dearly (see next paragraph). In *Academically Adrift*, Arum and Roksa (2011) laid out the academy's failure to educate in disturbing figures. For example, over four years, 36% of students showed no significant progress in learning, according to their Collegiate Learning Assessment (CLA) scores, and the progress that others showed was modest at best (less than half a standard deviation on the average). Specs grading could also improve the slipping status of the United States in the world ratings and rankings of student performance. In her evidence-rich book *The Smartest Kids in the World and How They Got That Way*, Amanda Ripley (2013) maintains that the primary reason why American education is faltering is its all-around lack of rigor—in the textbooks used, the quality of student work expected, and the grading standards. By contrast, Finland, South Korea, and Poland are rising in these student performance ratings and rankings, and she contends that their ascendency is the result of their academic rigor.

Rigor is a prickly subject these days. Many faculty honestly believe they are upholding it, and some are, but evidence suggests that there are too few, and for very good reasons that I will explain subsequently. In addition, rigor raises suspicion that it will deny disadvantaged, first-generation, and under-prepared students the chance to acquire—if they can even gain access to—higher education. This is a very important concern, but it masks the insulting assumption that these students could not cut it in a rigorous program. Tell that to the true *Stand and Deliver* (1988) hero, Jaime Escalante, who taught his at-risk high school students calculus. Tell that to any of the hundreds, if not thousands, of inner-city charter-school teachers. These students survived the worst of our K–12 education, and they *can* learn if they learn how to learn. The last section of chapter 6 of this book offers concrete strategies to teach them this without robbing time and attention from the course content.

Let us consider the currently sagging legitimacy and value of higher education, which ranks among the biggest challenges facing the academy. As chapter 1 documents, neither the employers of our college graduates nor the members of the public at large are impressed with our products. They push us to develop a widening array of hard and soft skills in our students: ethical, teaming, leadership, communication, presentation, analytical and critical thinking, "fuzzy" problem solving, quantitative reasoning, and visual literacy, among others. Although students quest after certifications and degrees (and the job-market edge they give), they are not particularly motivated to master the knowledge and skills we are trying to help them learn and sincerely believe are essential to their life success and fulfillment. Students fail to see the connections between our foci and their employment, or they just do not buy our argument linking them. Their skepticism is understandable given the direction of the economy. While Pew Research studies document that a bachelor's degree pays off more today in higher individual and household income than it ever did, controlling for inflation (Fry, 2014), students can counter that their loan repayments will undermine their gains and that all but the highest level incomes are falling as the economy fails to generate new jobs.

Greater educational rigor should go far to rebuild that legitimacy and value, especially with prospective employers and the public at large. Evidence abounds that it has faded into the background, and with it, learning. Faculty are not at fault here; they lack the power either to have instigated this trend or to stem it. But consider these recent academic policy changes. Many colleges and universities are dropping remedial curricula, and not because students are entering with stronger writing and mathematical skills. The reason given is that, because developmental courses carry no credit, they lengthen the college experience and discourage students from persisting. As a result, these institutions will start giving college credit for learning material that students should have mastered in high school and even earlier. Their instructors who teach nonremedial courses must take extra care not to mistake a student's poor preparation for low motivation. In addition, many institutions have made it easier for students to withdraw from courses in which they are not doing well in order to avoid a bad grade and then repeat those courses (called *forgiveness*).

The curriculum is not sacred anymore either—or completely faculty-driven. The Alamo Colleges administrations in Texas almost succeeded in replacing a three-credit humanities course with a student-success-plus-leadership course based in part on Stephen R. Covey's (2013) *The 7 Habits of Highly Effective People*—hardly as challenging as Plato or Dickens (Berrett, 2014a). The faculty protested and won with the support of the regional accreditor.

Another blow to rigor and learning comes from increasing class sizes. Larger classes are known to undermine student attendance, classroom civility, academic integrity, student motivation and performance, the acquisition of advanced thinking skills, retention of the material, college persistence, and student satisfaction with the course and the instructor, as well as faculty morale (Cuseo, 2007). Greater class size almost always means greater student heterogeneity in the class, which means a wider range of backgrounds in the course content. Yet we know that one of the most powerful determinants of learning is the student's background in the subject matter (Bransford, Brown, & Cocking, 2000). If students start a course with very different levels of prior knowledge, where is an instructor to aim? If he or she targets the middle, students with either a weak or a strong background are likely to learn less than they otherwise could. On the other hand, more students feed the bottom line and hold the promise (true or false) of more graduates.

Yet another eyebrow-raising trend in higher education has been grade inflation, now a well-established fact (Johnson, 2003; Rojstaczer & Healey, 2012), but at the same time our students have been devoting much less time and effort to their homework than they used to. Those in college full-time spend an average of only 15 hours a week on their out-of-class course work, which figures to about three hours per three-credit course per week. This discouraging statistic represents a marked decline from 50 years ago and holds true whether or not students are working while in school (Babcock & Marks, 2011). This means that they are spending much less time on task, and we know that more time on task leads to greater learning. Institutions designed their credit-hour-based four-year degree programs many decades ago at a time when few students were working. Now most of them are, some of them full-time. They cannot possibly dedicate to their studies the time they are supposed to. Yet they still graduate with decent, if not high, GPAs. It just may take them a year or two longer.

Perhaps the customer service model adopted by administrators and students has dealt rigor the knockout punch. This model prioritizes student satisfaction over student learning and positions degrees and certifications as commodities for sale. Having to work for them does not make much sense from a customer's point of view. You do not have to work for a car or a smartphone once you buy it, right? Furthermore, student customers expect faculty and student affairs personnel to provide top-quality service for all that tuition money. Outside the classroom, there should be plenty of clubs, activities, special programs, recreational opportunities, well-appointed residence halls, parking spaces, bandwidth, and sports. Inside, instructors should make learning as painless and entertaining as possible, return graded work overnight, and tailor teaching to individual student needs. Those who do not may collect complaints on the end-of-course student rating forms, and administrators take the negative scores and comments seriously. They are known to pay inordinate attention to the few disparaging remarks and overlook the majority of compliments. Because negative ratings adversely affect reappointment, tenure, and promotion decisions, some faculty do whatever is necessary to raise their numbers. This typically involves trimming the content and lowering standards so students receive higher grades with less effort. As history professor David M. Perry (2014) puts it:

> Tell faculty members that they are obligated to treat students like customers, and the instructors will either eschew rigor in favor of making satisfaction guaranteed or work defensively lest they be harangued by the irate customer. Tell students that they are consumers, and they will act like consumers but ultimately learn less and perhaps not even receive the credential that they think they are buying.

Faculty are in no position to counter all the powerful forces against rigor. But they can mount a peaceful resistance to them by holding students to high standards in their own classrooms and, better yet, across entire programs when they act as a group. They can set and enforce whatever expectations they can articulate clearly to their students and enable them to meet. Specs grading provides the framework for doing this without raising the ire of students.

Certainly we can and should spark up our courses with compelling learning experiences, engaging examples and stories, and friendly humor to motivate and facilitate our students' learning. In fact, because we find our discipline so entertaining, we can go far to make it enjoyable and rewarding for others. But we must also tell students that learning is inherently work, however satisfying, that they have to do in their own head. In addition, it can occasionally and unavoidably be painful for them to let go of their faulty beliefs and mind-sets. We must also inform students that they are not customers but clients and that clients have to hold up their end of the relationship. They are like patients who have to follow their physician's orders to get more tests, obtain and take medications, and modify their lifestyles to get good results. Similarly, lawyers require clients to furnish information and complete paperwork, and physical therapists assign their patients often painful exercises. We also must disavow students of the illusion that they just look up whatever they need to know on the web. All that information and data are useless without the ability to judge their value, interpret them, place them in context, and integrate them with other information and data. This ability is rooted in knowledge, which is a complex, evidence-based structure of the way the world works. One learns how to think *within* it until it becomes a habit of mind. This is what students can learn from us that they can learn nowhere else.

Linda B. Nilson
Anderson, SC
July 2014

ACKNOWLEDGMENTS

So many people have contributed to this book. My gratitude goes to those who shared their grading experiences with a new type of grading and, really, course design. Some shared by publishing or posting on the web their syllabi or summaries of their experiences. Others shared more directly by sending or handing me their course documents and letting me probe further with specific questions. I thank the following individuals for every minute of their help: Risa Applegarth (University of North Carolina at Greensboro); Jeffrey Appling, Dianna Conley, Janet Craig, Steve Davis (retired), Jennifer Goree, Ardi Kinerd, Janice Lanham, Will Mayo, Janis L. Miller, June J. Pilcher, Susan Pope, Mike Pulley, Cynthia Pury, D. E. ("Steve") Stevenson, Wayne Stewart, and William Terry (all at Clemson University); Cathy Davidson (Duke University); Laura Gibbs (University of Oklahoma); Kathleen Kegley (Synchlora Management Consulting; formerly University of Maryland University College and Clemson University); Laurence L. Leff (Western Illinois University); Jeffrey M. Ringer (University of Tennessee, Knoxville; formerly Lee University); Michael J. Strada (West Liberty State University; retired); and Susan Waldenberger (Pima Community College).

Of these wonderful fellow academics, I am most deeply indebted to Dr. Kathy Kegley, from whom many of the ideas in this book originated. Now a creativity consultant, Kathy was the kind of instructor who was always seeking a better way to teach and experimenting with novel ways of doing things. And I mean *novel*. She did not pick up instructional fads, and there are always plenty of them floating around. No, she *invented* new solutions to challenges. In fact, she is the most creative individual I know personally.

Kathy found deducting points from her students' work and writing justifications for it distasteful. So she devised a new and different way to assess students: discarding points entirely and bundling assignments so students could choose their own workload and grade. By telling students up front exactly what they had to do for each grade, she found that they regarded themselves, not her, responsible for their grades and no longer complained about them. In addition, they never disappointed her by falling short of her expectations, so her comments could focus on strengths and possible improvements and not even bring up the grade. Many of her students remarked that they had never received so much feedback from an instructor. They probably had, but comments tied to the grade encourage students to strategize on winning back points rather than "hearing" the instructor's feedback. Her feedback was bureaucratically "unnecessary" and freely given with the purest of good intentions. So her students paid attention to it—and they richly benefited.

I am forever grateful that Kathy shared her innovative approach with me. She did not think it was that special, but I knew right away that it was. I saw its potential for rigor and efficiency in its implicit pass/fail standards. Later I explored the related literature, considered how parts of her approach could accommodate a point system, and added value by linking it to learning outcomes, thereby bridging the gap between assessment and grading. She and I refined the emerging grading system together by developing and facilitating workshops on it, learning from the participants, and devoting hours of face-to-face and virtual conversations about it over several years. Our original plan was to collaborate on this book, but she took her life in another direction and handed the project entirely to me. I have run with it because I believe it holds tremendous promise to solve many of the problems facing faculty, students, and higher education in general.

One other person who made this book possible was my editor/publisher, John von Knorring. A few years ago, he reviewed a proposal for it with earlier versions of three or four chapters. He rejected it largely because he did not think a market for the book existed at that time. He was no doubt right; another publisher had rejected it for being "too radical." Then, competency-based education and assessment started getting a great deal of positive press and support in many higher education circles. Perhaps the time for this book was coming! John encouraged me to give a session on the grading system at the 2013 conference of the Professional and Organization Development (POD) Network in Higher Education, and it was very well received. The time *had* arrived, but the book was still risky. He decided to take a chance on it anyway. I cannot thank him enough.

Consider yourself fortunate if you ever get to work with John. This is my second book with Stylus, and his judgment has proven impeccable. His suggestions for revisions have always made sense, even those few that spurred a discussion leading us to another resolution. He has an uncanny way of knowing what is missing in a book and what can enhance it. He can take the role of the readers and anticipate their questions. And he provides his feedback quickly, so you still remember where your head was when you wrote the text he has commented on. Somehow he finds time to represent Stylus at an endless list of conferences and bike hundreds of miles each year.

My dear colleague Dannelle D. Stevens carefully reviewed an earlier version of the manuscript and provided amazingly helpful comments and suggestions to make it clearer and more useful to faculty. She also said what was *good* about it. As I imagined her telling her students the best features of their work, her words made me glow like a proud student!

My fall 2013 and spring 2014 writing groups also merit my thanks because having to report my progress on this book every two weeks spurred me on to give this work the steady and focused attention it deserved.

Finally, I am grateful to my dear husband, Greg Bauernfeind, who continues to believe in me and respects the time I spend away from him to research and write. He is not and never was an academic, so his patience and understanding of the mental, emotional, and physical demands of this strange industry have amazed me for years. He really wants to know how my latest project is going and celebrates with me when it is going well. It is hard to say what professional work I would get done if he were not encouraging me and lightening the load of household tasks. He has been integral to any success I have enjoyed.

THE NEED FOR A NEW GRADING SYSTEM

Imagining higher education without grades of any kind may sound like an exercise in fantasy, but, in fact, grades did not always exist. The roots of the university date back to 6th-century Europe, when monastic and cathedral-based schools first appeared. In the high medieval period, some of them assumed university status, the first of which was the University of Bologna, founded in 1088. As far as we know, neither these new institutions nor the schools that spawned them graded their students' performance.

Something like grades was instituted just three centuries ago when European universities started fostering competitions among students for prizes and rank order. No competition was fiercer than the Cambridge Mathematical Tripos examination, begun in the early 1700s and increasingly formalized during the 18th century. It took the form of a tournament in which correct answers to questions moved students up the rungs and the ranking system. As they rose, students faced more challenging questions and more able opponents. The Tripos went on for days and offered compelling rewards. The top competitors received "titles" that they carried with them through adulthood and substantial amounts of money. The most successful student shared in a portion of the institution's endowment for life. Conversely, the poorest competitors suffered long-term dishonor (Schneider & Hutt, 2013).

Apparently, the Tripos served as the model for the American grading system (Schneider & Hutt, 2013). In 1783, Ezra Stiles, president of Yale University, introduced an achievement-based student ranking and classification system using Latin descriptors, from the outstanding *optime* to the failing *pejores*. By 1800, Yale dropped the Latin designations and adopted a numerical scale of 0–4, paving the way for the grade point average (GPA). The College of William & Mary soon followed suit. The University of Michigan initiated a pass/fail system in 1850 that set the passing bar at a low 50%. But these were individual institutional actions, not standard-setting innovations. Grading practices were developed later in the century when colleges and universities across the country began imitating Harvard's new letter-grade system. However, this hallowed institution set passing at a mere 26%. Michigan maintained its 50% standard while Mount Holyoke upped the ante to 75% (Hammons & Barnsley, 1992).

The academy eventually closed the gaps in the scale and adopted the letter system as the standard. Some institutions added +/– modifiers. In the criterion-referenced grading system, each letter grade came to represent a designated standard, with A meaning a percentage score in the 90s of total possible points, B signifying a score in the 80s, C one in the 70s, D one in the 60s, and F one below 60. In norm-referenced grading, commonly known as "grading on a curve," the letters might indicate almost any score range, depending on the performance of a class as a whole. Some faculty reserved an A for the top 10% of scores and others for the top 20%. There were and still are no hard-and-fast rules.

In theory, educators agree that an A should signify an exceptional level of achievement. The student should have to display a superb command of the subject matter and the ability to apply, analyze, evaluate, and even create with it. A grade of B is supposed to indicate a good but not outstanding level of achievement—that is, at least a solid grasp of the material and the ability to perform some higher-order cognitive operations on it. A grade of C should represent a fair level of achievement, implying some mastery of most of the material and perhaps some ability to use it. But theory does not guarantee corresponding practice. Grade inflation and the varying interpretations that institutions and individual faculty attach to grades have eroded these meanings.

This chapter reviews what grades have come to signify and the behaviors they have generated among the several parties concerned: employers, institutions, faculty, and students. As will be shown, no matter which perspective we take, the grading system that higher education in the United States has relied on for many decades has serious problems. It does not work in anyone's interests, and it genuinely hurts those most directly associated with it: the faculty and the students. In fact, the system is broken.

Traditional Grading and Employers

Not long ago, a group of researchers (Samson, Graue, Weinstein, & Walberg, 1984) conducted a meta-analysis of 35 studies on the relationship between college grades, indicated by GPA, and occupational success, measured as career position, job satisfaction, income, performance rating, and combinations of these and related variables. Faculty would expect students' college performance to predict at least moderately well students' real-world success after graduation. Yet Samson et al. found that the study-weighted mean of 209 correlations between GPA and occupational success was only 0.155. Although statistically significant, grades and academic test scores accounted for only 2.4% of the variance in career success. In other words, the academy's grading criteria proved only weakly related to the abilities, knowledge, and dispositions that the U.S. occupational structure values and rewards.

This research was published years before the term *student learning outcomes* entered the academic vocabulary. Now, outcomes provide the backbone of courses, programs, and entire curricula, and many of these outcomes are job related, such as "The student will be able to organize, document, and write a product development proposal that a real corporation would deem acceptable"; "The student will be able to work effectively as part of a team"; and "The student will be able to interview patients from diverse cultures, specifically to obtain accurate, detailed information on their family history, current medications, and immediate condition." The next chapter provides a primer on how to write assessable learning outcomes and how to design a course around them to maximize the chances that students will achieve them.

Employers take note of the grades of the graduates who make the first or second cut for a position. They hope that a relatively high GPA in the major and overall ensures high competency in both the technical and the softer skills of the job in question. Unfortunately, they are often disappointed. Many larger companies have established their own remedial "colleges" that not only orient new hires to the company's policies, standard operating procedures, and technical peculiarities, but also train them in basic communication and quantitative skills.

Traditional Grading and Institutions of Higher Learning

In spite of the emphasis on preparing students for employment, higher education is not just a white-collar vocational school. Many courses and curricula, general education included, promise student outcomes that have nothing to do with jobs directly. Examples of such outcomes include: "The student will be able to judge the scientific validity of claims made in the mass media or find resources that will allow competent judgments of the claims"; "The student will be able to identify and articulate the various positions in the assigned literature and draw sound comparisons and contrasts among them"; and "The student will develop the listening, cognitive, and social skills to engage in open, civil, intellectual discussion of controversial social issues." Indeed, the mission of higher education extends beyond producing dependable and skilled workers. It also strives to develop responsible citizens, competent readers and writers, discriminating consumers, wise life-decision makers, and meaning-seeking human beings.

Even though outcomes supposedly guide higher education, institutions assess the actual extent to which students have achieved them only at the program and curricular levels. And even then, the assessment process and standards are murky. If students are supposed to achieve 10 general-education outcomes and 30 program outcomes before they graduate, does the fact that they receive their college diploma at commencement mean that they are actually competent in *all* the abilities represented by *all* the outcomes? The evidence leans against it. For example, almost every college and university promises good communication skills as an outcome, but many college graduates cannot even read well, let alone communicate effectively orally or in writing. According to a 2006 study by the American Institutes for Research, fewer than half the students graduating from four-year colleges and fewer than three fourths of those graduating from two-year colleges demonstrate literary proficiency.

Outcome assessment is even more tenuous at the course level, where grades and ultimately GPAs are determined. Grades do not directly assess whether or not students have attained outcome X or Y or Z. At best, they reflect the *degree* to which students have achieved the course outcomes *in general*. Has a student who earned an A in a course achieved *all* of the learning outcomes at an *exceptionally high* level of competency or merely at a *satisfactory* level? The majority of students getting a final grade of B, C, or D present even more ambiguous cases. Did they attain some of the outcomes at a satisfactory level and not others? Did they achieve a few at a high level of competency and others not at all? At what level did they achieve any of them? It is impossible to tell, and the syllabus probably does not translate course grades into demonstrated skills either. As a result, institutions must take the additional time-consuming steps to assess students' competencies at the program and curricular levels to meet accreditation and accountability requirements.

The problem is that faculty march to the beat of a different drummer. They simply penalize students who fail to achieve learning outcomes at the desired level by giving them a lower grade. So a passing grade in a course does not certify competency in *any* of the outcomes. Some faculty may want to fail students who demonstrate little or no competency but would get in trouble with their chairs and deans for failing too many. Unless students stop coming to class, provide too few means of assessment, or demonstrate absurdly low competency, they generally pass. Moreover, the assignments and tests used for calculating the course grade may have only tenuous connections to outcomes. If faculty were evaluating student performance explicitly on the basis of outcomes achievement, the grading scale would have to map grades onto outcomes.

Generally, student learning outcomes imply "can" or "cannot" determinations. If students are supposed be able to do something at an acceptable level by the end of the semester, they either can or cannot do it. But what is an acceptable or satisfactory level? Faculty rarely discuss or set such a level in their syllabi, tests, or assignment instructions. A grade of C implies *acceptable* but does not translate into the achievement of outcomes.

Traditional Grading and the Faculty

Aside from the fact that traditional grades tell us little about student competencies—a matter of much concern to employers—they bog down faculty with unnecessarily time-consuming and unpleasant work burdens.

One such time-eater relates to partial credit. In the current grading system, instructors are expected to give partial credit for almost anything correct a student submits, including largely wrong or vague responses. Perhaps they fear that giving zeros for poor work might discourage students or lead to their failing more students (which administrators discourage); or maybe they are happy to get *any* work out of their students. In any case, determining how many points of the possible maximum to allocate to a given answer is never easy. In their effort to be fair, faculty often go back over assignments and tests they have already graded to find out how they scored a similar response. Then they feel obliged to justify whatever points they subtract by writing on the student's work what is inaccurate, illogical, or missing in the work or even reteaching the correct approach. When we multiply this effort by the number of test questions or writing assignments and the number of students in their classes, it becomes clear why so many faculty shy away from substantial writing assignments and essay tests. Rubrics significantly reduce the burden, but instructors still spend a great deal of time grading.

Today faculty simply lack the time to conduct the most appropriate assessments. They are under pressure to do more research and service than ever before, and they are shouldering progressively heavier course loads of increasingly larger undergraduate classes. No wonder so many succumb to test bank–based objective exams. At the same time, their students demand more and more frequent assessments, while their administrators push them to teach and assess more complex skills, such as critical thinking and research abilities.

Another trend that can add to the faculty workload is the current emphasis on "authentic assessment," which is graded work that reflects real-world problem solving and typical job activities. This type of assessment characterizes undergraduate major and graduate courses in particular, the latter of which are increasingly offered online and commonly have no proctored exams. In this context, assessment must usually require students to construct some sort of product, such as a report, proposal, diagram, design, program, or multimedia presentation, all of which entail considerable time to grade.

What the faculty reap for their endless hours of grading are more grading protests and conflicts with students than ever before. Of course, the reasons behind this student behavior lie largely in the values and beliefs of the Millennial generation and their parents, such as their customer attitude toward higher education, their distaste for academic learning and the life of the mind, their alienation from standard teaching methods, and their sense of entitlement to high grades in light of high tuition costs. Instructors who understand these motivations can use any of several methods to stem the nuisance complaints about grades (Nilson, 2010). But traditional grading, which is so reliant on partial credit and hair-splitting point allocation, actually encourages students with a Millennial mentality to fight for extra points whenever they see a possible opening. Naturally, they would not bother with this strategy if it did not work at least some of the time.

Dr. Kathleen Kegley, a management consultant and former lecturer in Clemson University's MBA program and the University of Maryland University College's Information Technology program, recalls how she used to feel using the traditional, point-based, partial-credit method:

> The passion I had for teaching was being killed by the dread I continuously faced with grading and worse, handing back the graded assignments. I found the after-grade encounters often antagonistic and more often related to winning back points than understanding the lessons to be learned from the experience. (personal communication, October 17, 2010)

The current grading system has also exacerbated, though did not cause, the problems of grade inflation and sinking academic performance standards. These developed out of various changes in the academy and the broader society: multilevel government pressure on the academy to accept and graduate more students; institutional competition to attract and retain more students;

fierce competition for high national rankings (determined in part by applicant rejection rates and first-year student retention rates); students' poor preparation for college; students' widespread Millennial values and beliefs (as just discussed); the increasing importance of student ratings, which measure customer satisfaction, in faculty reviews and rewards (Nilson, 2012); and the widespread faculty belief that lenient grading generates higher student ratings (Nilson, 2009). This environment prioritizes credentials over learning, results over the integrity of the process, and student satisfaction over rigor and achievement of excellence. It also inclines faculty to adapt their content, standards, and grades to the attitudes, interests, work ethic, and skill levels that the students bring to college. These adjustments increase the odds of students passing courses, staying in school, not complaining, and evaluating instructors favorably.

Traditional Grading and Students

Given the social and political context in which higher education operates today, it would seem that the current grading system serves students quite well. Indeed, it does serve their short-term, pragmatic interests. But though they may not know it yet, students pay the steep costs with their mental health, learning, enjoyment of the college experience, cognitive development, and lifelong learning skills.

The partial-credit point system turns grades—and really all college course work—into a game, the object of which is to maximize the number of points toward one's grade with the lowest possible investment of time and effort. This is especially true for traditional-age students (Benton, 2006; Nathan, 2005; Singleton-Jackson, Jackson, & Reinhardt, 2010). Still, students believe that this game has a critical impact on their future career and earning power, so they play it very seriously. Therefore, regardless of their academic commitment and the amount of work they put into their courses, they are stressed about their grades. The evidence for this stress is compelling. Consider the most recent findings of the American College Health Association (2013, pp. 14–16):

- Fifty-one percent of students reported feeling "overwhelming anxiety" and almost 13% were diagnosed or treated by a professional for anxiety within the previous year.
- More than 31% reported feeling "so depressed that it was difficult to function" and 11% were diagnosed or treated by a professional for depression within the previous year.

- Six percent were diagnosed or treated by a professional for panic attacks within the previous year.
- Almost 42% rated their overall level of stress as "more than average," and more than 10% as "tremendous" within the previous year.
- Forty-five percent reported feeling "things were hopeless" within the previous year.
- Almost 84% reported feeling "overwhelmed" by all they had to do within the previous year.
- Almost 45% reported finding academics "traumatic or very difficult to handle" within the previous year.

Of course, student anxiety and depression have many sources, but "academics" took first place among all of them, being "traumatic or very difficult to handle" for many more students than career-related issues, family problems, intimate relationships, finances, and sleep difficulties.

This stress gives rise to "grade-grubbing," which translates into students' frequently protesting their grades and pressuring faculty to give them more points, even when not justified. Two other popular tactics for "winning the game" are cheating and plagiarism. In recent surveys, the majority of students have freely and even guiltlessly admitted to lifting text and answers for their daily homework, tests, and major assignments from unauthorized sources (Berry, Thornton, & Baker, 2006; Center for Academic Integrity as cited in Hutton, 2006; Kellogg, 2002; Kleiner & Lord, 1999).

If the current grading system turns college into a somewhat mean-spirited game, it obviously does not inspire students' motivation to learn. In fact, it seems to undercut their interest in the material. Nor does it seem to further their desire to improve their performance. Many students ignore much of the faculty's feedback on their work and see it as little more than a justification for taking off points.

For all the gamelike tactics students use to raise their grades, many of them, especially those from middle- and upper-middle-class homes, feel little sense of responsibility for their learning or their performance (Singleton-Jackson et al., 2010). Their parents and K–12 teachers have generously praised them for their intelligence, fostering either the belief that they should excel no matter how little effort they invest or the fear that challenging tasks may compromise their self-esteem (Levine & Dean, 2012). Either way, they often see their grades—at least their bad grades (which could be a B)—as beyond their control. This thinking leaves two possible explanations for unfavorable grades: They reflect the unrealistic standards held by out-of-touch or ill-intended instructors, who additionally may be teaching irrelevant or too-advanced material ("*You* gave me a C!"); or they are a curse of fate. Both attributions belie students' belief in an external, as opposed to internal, locus of control (Dweck, 2007; Glenn, 2010a) and reinforce their cynical view of faculty feedback. Some disadvantaged students espouse another version of fatalism: the paralyzing belief that they do not belong in this strange culture of higher education and any poor or mediocre grades they get "prove" it. It is incumbent on faculty both to combat complacency and to recognize when students have genuine need for support.

While traditional grading cannot directly explain students' perceptions that external forces largely determine their grades, it certainly does little to alter them. However, a good grading system *should* make students feel that they are in the driver's seat of their education, and that their time, effort, and creativity will produce the results that will earn them good grades.

Criteria for Evaluating Grading Systems

In so many ways our current grading system leaves much to be desired. But we have not yet formalized how to appraise a grading system or what we want to see in one. What would a better system offer that we are not getting now? Of course, it should be feasible and fairly easy to implement. Let's not even try to overturn institutional standard operating procedures such as giving final letter grades. Although some of us may be uncomfortable with the A–F scale, only institutions can change it—not faculty. Besides, final letter grades do not present the problems that our current way of judging student work does.

We can identify some criteria for evaluating grading systems by sorting through the adverse unintended consequences of our current practices:

1. *Uphold high academic standards.* We have seen that our current system incentivizes faculty to sacrifice rigor in order to enhance student satisfaction and avoid administrative censure for giving too many low grades. In turn, students fail to master much content, refine their skills, maximize their cognitive development, and adopt lifelong learning skills. Their employers also suffer by having to hire and manage graduates who are ill prepared in communication, collaboration, analytical thinking, and problem solving.

A better system would establish and maintain high standards for student work, restoring integrity to grades and reflecting discriminating professional judgment. (Also see criterion 4, "Motivate students to excel.") At the same time, it would not lower an instructor's student ratings.

2. *Reflect student learning outcomes.* Unfortunately, grades as we know them today do not reflect the learning outcomes that the students have and have not achieved. After all, either a student achieves a given outcome or he doesn't. In this context, what does a D, C, or B mean? Has a student achieved

some of the outcomes? If so, which ones? Has he actually achieved *any* of them? Or does he merely fail at a higher level than he did at the beginning of the course? No wonder employers and accrediting agencies put little stock in grades. As a result, students really do not know what they are capable of and probably assume they have mastered the outcomes well enough. Besides, the word *outcome* sounds like something that has already happened.

In a better grading system, grades would be tied to results—specifically, what outcomes of the course students have and have not achieved—and the relationship between grades and outcomes achievement could be easily explained in a syllabus. This means that course grades could be related to program outcomes.

3. *Motivate students to learn.* As elaborated earlier, our current system has turned higher education into a game that students win when they obtain the most coveted rewards—that is, high grades—for putting in the least amount of time and effort. Desirable grades are not only the coin of the realm but also, students believe, a key to a better occupational and economic future. Performance, then, is everything; learning does not even figure into the game.

Ideally, a grading system would emphasize learning over grades and encourage a learning over a performance orientation (Dweck & Leggett, 1988). Students would *want* to learn, and, given well-designed assessment instruments, grades would closely mirror learning.

4. *Motivate students to excel.* As we have seen, allocating partial credit for less than satisfactory work discourages students from aspiring to achieve excellence. In fact, it lowers the marginal utility of moving beyond a minimal investment of time and effort. It lets students slip by in their course work and thereby win the higher education game.

A better grading system would build in incentives for students to aim high, work hard, and do their best. It would demand strong performances to earn any points and would make inferior work unacceptable.

5. *Discourage cheating.* In the current grading system, cheating and plagiarism are popular strategies that some students use to help them win the higher education game. With little incentive to learn or do high-quality work, why shouldn't they cheat and plagiarize? In fact, some students put considerable time, effort, and even money into implementing these strategies and eluding detection. They may regard this as part of the game.

An improved system would make cheating either more difficult, less appealing, or both. It would rely more on authentic assessments, focus on developing higher-order cognitive skills and creativity, do a better job of motivating students to learn and excel, or furnish them with more choices and control over their learning and assessment.

6. *Reduce student stress.* Apparently, our system is hazardous to our students' mental health. In the game of higher education, students stress over

a low grade because it may affect their precarious future job prospects and financial well-being. Their anxiety increases when they fail to understand instructors' expectations of their work and feel they lack control over their academic success.

Even the most ideal grading system could not *eliminate* student stress, but a better system would give students a stronger sense of control over their educational lives, a clearer picture of faculty expectations, more choice and volition, and a more accurate handle on what they can and cannot do at satisfactory levels. It would also minimize grade-related conflicts with their instructors.

7. *Make students feel responsible for their grades.* With our current grading system, some students blame their lower than expected grades on an external locus of control, such as the fates or their instructors. They may not understand faculty expectations, or they may bank on eking a few more points out of weary instructors.

It would be better to grade within a system that would give students clear choices about how much and how deeply to master the course material and tie their choices to their grades. As long as they know what they have to do for each grade, students would realize that the responsibility for earning that grade rests squarely on them. No doubt an unfavorable grade would not damage an instructor's student ratings to the extent that it does now.

8. *Minimize conflict between faculty and students.* The higher education game that our current grading system fosters is a high-stakes one. Students' stress over grades gives rise to grade-grubbing, which translates into their frequently protesting their grades and pressuring faculty to give them more points, even when not justified. This ritualized conflict harms the rapport and trust between students and faculty and robs them both of productive time.

In a better grading system, students would understand the work required for each assignment and test as well as their central role in determining their grades. Therefore, they would stop confronting their instructors with grade protests and hopefully evaluate their faculty more gently.

Another unpleasant interaction that students have with faculty is negotiating an extension on an assignment. After all, everything is negotiable, right? An improved system would incorporate positive incentives for students to plan ahead and submit work on time or even early. At the same time, it would build in automatic costs for students who choose to take an extension, and it would be clearly their choice to do so, not the instructor's discretion.

9. *Save faculty time.* Unless an instructor relies on objective items from a test bank, grading takes an enormous amount of time these days, even for faculty using rubrics. Furthermore, it is time unpleasantly spent. Grading is arduous: reading difficult-to-understand prose, passing judgments, working through disappointments, parceling out partial credit, and justifying these

decisions in writing to suspicious students. And grading offers no happy ending. Faculty know that the results will ultimately drive a wedge between them and at least some of their students, and that they will have to spend more time adjudicating grade complaints.

There is a better way, one that would free instructors from endless, mind-numbing hours of writing justifications and explanations on their students' work. It would not give partial credit, nor would it have graduated levels of performance. Rather, it would rely on simple, one-level rubrics anchored in demonstrating achievement of outcomes.

10. *Give students feedback they will use.* Currently, students seem to view faculty feedback on their work primarily as justifications for the grade and not so much as constructive advice on how to improve next time.

In a better system, faculty would not have to justify taking off points and splitting hairs of quality. Students might then regard the feedback they receive from their instructors as intended to be constructive and useful.

These 10 criteria for evaluating a grading system grew out of our current system's flaws, but additional standards apply as well:

11. *Make expectations clear.* Today's grading system does not obscure faculty standards and expectations, but it does not induce instructors to write particularly detailed directions either. Consequently, students often complain that faculty do not supply enough information on what they are looking for in an assignment or test and how they will assess it. Although rubrics describe the various performance levels of student-constructed work, the descriptions are usually quite brief—short enough to fit in a tabular cell—and minor homework assignments may or may not have instructions and a rubric.

In an ideal grading system, the faculty's most time-consuming and detail-oriented task would be writing or scripting their expectations, standards, and directions for assignments and tests so as to communicate them clearly to their students. This may mean checking students' comprehension by having them paraphrase back those expectations or grade a work sample against them. In any case, students would understand what they need to do to get any given grade in each assignment and the course overall. As we have seen, many of the characteristics of an ideal grading system rest on this clarity.

12. *Foster higher-order cognitive development and creativity.* Again, nothing in our current system directly inhibits faculty from teaching and assessing higher-order cognitive skills, such as applying, analyzing, evaluating, and creating. But the system does discourage them because it makes grading so time-consuming. Whereas objective test items can be written to assess higher-order thinking (Suskie, 2004), test-bank items are rarely designed to do so, which passes on to faculty the task of composing such items. Otherwise,

faculty must give assignments that require students to "construct" something on their own—an essay, a paper, a visual representation, a portfolio, a written or oral translation, a computer program, an engineering or graphics design, a multimedia project, or a piece of art—that would require and demonstrate higher-order thinking to be considered a worthy product.

Obviously, a better system would allow faculty to grade student-constructed work more easily and quickly. Relying on a one-level rubric would probably accomplish this.

13. *Assess authentically.* Students preparing for or already pursuing a career rightfully expect to learn skills and do assignments that are "authentic"—that is, "real world" and "career related," which are qualities that typical multiple-choice tests lack. Adult and advanced students in particular demand authenticity. Many of these students are taking online courses, where proctored exams are impossible and only student-constructed work is appropriate.

But grading authentic assessments in our current system presents the same problems for faculty—considerable time and effort—as does grading assessments of higher-order cognitive skills. An ideal grading system would streamline this assessment process for faculty.

14. *Have high interrater agreement.* In general, the greater the number of rating gradations, the finer they are, and the more room there is for disagreement among raters. This is especially true when the expectations for the work are not completely clear or sufficiently detailed, which is sometimes a problem in today's grading system. Standardized testing companies go to great lengths to ensure interrater consistency by training their raters of essays to use a rubric in a uniform way.

A better grading system would allow fewer options and less room for disagreement. It might have as few as two rating options, satisfactory or unsatisfactory, and would emphasize explicating clear criteria for a satisfactory performance. That is, the assessment standards would be clear enough that disciplinary colleagues would typically agree on their rating of given student products.

15. *Be simple.* A grading system like the one we most commonly use now has too many rating levels for too many individual assignments and tests based on too elaborate a point structure to be considered simple. No wonder students ask so many questions about how they will be graded in a course and so often forget the details. Even instructors get confused.

Streamlining the grading procedures as criterion 14 suggests would improve the system for all parties involved. By "chunking" aspects of a course, both instructors and students would find it easier to recall the criteria for final grades. For instance, we might group assignments into bundles or modules around learning outcomes and course grades. We could also simplify the point system and faculty decision making by eliminating partial credit and using a one-level rubric.

Why Not Try a New Approach?

Everyone touched by our current grading system—employers, institutions, faculty, and students—encounters serious academic and practical problems with it. These flaws may run too deep to patch the system with small-scale modifications. The issue is not with letter grades per se. As history shows, they can mean anything the academy agrees to. The alternative practice of copious, faculty-written descriptions of each student's performance in each course, made famous at Reed College and in the past at the University of California at Santa Cruz, only creates new practical challenges. It multiplies everyone's workload except the students' and would be impossible in larger classes.

If today's system is indeed broken, it needs to be replaced with a new and better one that avoids or at least mitigates the drawbacks of the old one. This book describes a grading system that, when implemented properly, accomplishes this and rates more favorably on the 15 criteria for evaluating grading systems just presented. This new approach borrows elements of pass/fail grading, competency-based education, and classic contract grading, and incorporates opportunities for student choice and control that boost motivation and sense of responsibility. It also depends on a sound course design—that is, a design anchored in clear, assessable student learning outcomes that are sequentially organized into a logical, cohesive learning process. The design then informs the development and selection of appropriate assessments and the most effective instructional strategies. So the next chapter offers a brief tutorial in the best course design and development practices and lists research-based resources that treat the topic in great depth and detail.

Chapter 3 explains how we can tie students' course grades to their achievement (or lack thereof) of learning outcomes. In effect, students receive credit toward their final grade based on the *number* of work requirements and the *specific* work requirements they complete at a satisfactory level by given due dates. In other words, students earn higher grades by jumping *more* hurdles that show evidence of *more* learning (greater amount or breadth of knowledge or greater number of skills) or jumping *higher* hurdles that show evidence of *more advanced* learning, or both. Higher hurdles may mean demonstrating higher-order cognitive skills, more advanced levels of cognitive development, higher levels of critical thinking, or the ability to solve more complex problems. A variety of course examples illustrate grading on more hurdles, others grading on higher hurdles, and still others grading on both criteria.

Chapter 4 assesses the efficacy of pass/fail grading on the levels of the course, assignments and tests within a course, and the program, which includes competency-based education. Pass/fail grading of assignments and tests has received strong support from faculty who have adopted the practice and have published their results. In addition, competency-based education is gaining ground as it proves itself across disparate institutions.

Chapter 5 introduces the term *specifications* (or *specs*) *grading* to identify a new grading system that relies on pass/fail grading of course components, such as assignments and tests. After elaborating on the idea of specifications, including how they relate to rubrics, it provides guidance on how to write specs for all kinds of assignments, from short and simple to long and complex to creative, and offers real examples. To balance the rigor of this new system, we explore ways to add flexibility and second chances with a token system or opportunities for students to revise or drop unacceptable work. Finally, we conduct an initial evaluation of specs grading against the 15 criteria developed earlier in this first chapter.

Chapter 6 explains how to convert specs-graded student work into final letter grades. Instructors have a choice: they can retain the point system and just add up the points that students accumulate across the quizzes, tests, and assignments in a course, or they can take the more innovative alternative of grouping assessments into several bundles or modules, each of which is associated with a final letter grade for the course. *Bundling* can streamline the grading structure and process as well as increase the learning value of standard assignments. The chapter offers several solid pedagogical reasons for bundling and proposes ways of tying bundles and modules to outcomes. Later sections delve into ways that we can help students, including those at risk, to do well in a specs-graded course. We also examine the likelihood of grade inflation with specs grading, comparing and contrasting it with different versions of contract grading, which *can* lead to grade inflation.

Having laid out the main characteristics of specs grading, we look at selected examples of this system from real college and university courses in chapter 7. The text points out features in the syllabi that previous chapters described and illustrates the wide variety of courses that have built in specs grading or something very much like it.

In chapter 8, we hear from more instructors about how the specs grading system worked for them and their classes and explain why the system enhances students' motivation to learn and to excel without evoking student complaints. According to classic theories of motivation, offering students choices should enhance their sense of self-determination, self-efficacy, control, and volition, which in turn should increase their motivation and encourage them to assume responsibility for their performance. A course using specs grading does this and allows considerable opportunity for student choice and control. The chapter details those opportunities and encourages integrating as many as possible.

Drawing on the experience of pioneering faculty, chapter 9 offers directions and advice to instructors who wish to implement this new grading strategy in a face-to-face, online, or hybrid course. It recommends strategies for designing a *pure* specs grading course and a *synthetic* specs grading course, which incorporates aspects of both specs and traditional grading. It also advises how to introduce specifications grading to students so that they appreciate the learning approach behind it and its benefits to them.

The book concludes with a brief chapter that thoroughly assesses all facets of specs grading against the 15 criteria for evaluating a grading system.

2

LEARNING OUTCOMES AND COURSE DESIGN

The literature on course design generally endorses the principles reviewed in this chapter. They facilitate ways of promoting and assessing student learning that generate the data that accrediting agencies require of programs and institutions. They also make developing a course a more logical and streamlined process for faculty. Readers already familiar with outcomes-based course design can skip this chapter.

Student Learning Outcomes

A learning outcome is an observable ability or skill that a student is supposed to acquire by the end of a learning unit, whether that is a program, course, course unit, period of time, or class session. Less formally, it is what students should be able *to do* by such-and-such a time. Verbs that describe internal states of mind (e.g., *know, realize, understand, appreciate,* or just plain *learn*) do not produce an action or a product that can be seen, read, heard, touched, smelled, or tasted. Therefore, they do not belong in learning outcomes. Instructors who are tempted to use such verbs should ask themselves exactly *how* they want their students to *know* or *understand*, how they want students to *demonstrate* that knowledge or understanding. Do they want students to be able to *recognize* concepts, terms, principles, and so on in objective items; do they want students to *reproduce* this knowledge, which means memorizing it or being able to express it in one's own words; or do they want students to be able to *apply* the knowledge in some way, perhaps to solve a problem? These are very different cognitive operations, and they dictate different study techniques and teaching methods.

Writing good learning outcomes forces faculty to figure out what they really want students to learn how to do. The verbs to use describe *actions,* even if the actions are largely mental. Actions can produce an observable *deliverable.* For example, recognizing concepts and principles can generate answers on an objective test. Reproductions of material can appear in a written or oral short answer, written essay, drawing, or graphic. Applying knowledge can mean providing examples, solving a problem, or debriefing a case, all of which can be written or spoken. Analyzing may take the form of a compare-and-contrast matrix, concept or mind map, Venn diagram, process flowchart, or graphic organizer, in addition to an essay or oral presentation. Creating may involve writing, designing, composing, cooking, performing, choreographing, recording, drawing, painting, sculpting, or solving a novel problem, and all of these actions generate products that are assessable through one or more senses. Evaluating, judging, or defending are evident in writing or presenting an argument, a diagnosis, a review, or an assessment. True, these mental operations are abstract, but they can be expressed and made visible. A lengthy list of student performance verbs that vary from low to high cognitive level is available in Nilson (2010).

Students want to know what skills and abilities they will gain from a course if they do the required work. So the syllabus should contain at least the more macrolevel learning outcomes. For instance, an operations management course syllabus may state that by the middle of the course students will be able to use well-established professional tools to analyze a company's operational processes and systems. However, the ability to execute this skill requires these and other microlevel skills as well: identifying and mitigating bottlenecks, locating the variability factors and assessing their impact, determining the most cost-effective levels of inventory ordering, and calculating return on investment. Instructors may or may not choose to put these skills in the syllabus. They know that too much text will discourage students from reading any of it.

Outcomes and Assessments

Once instructors develop a set of clear, assessable learning outcomes, their assessments—that is, what the assignments, quizzes, and tests should ask their students to do—are right in front of them. Outcomes are meant to be assessed, if not graded, and assessments should mirror the outcomes. If we want students to be able to solve differential equations, write a sonnet, explain how information technology can increase a company's strategic advantage, identify key similarities and differences between one war and another, or prepare treatment plans for diabetes patients at various stages of the disease, we have to have them do these exact things so we can assess how well they can do them.

A detailed outcome also describes the conditions, medium, setting, or special requirements of the assessment. Will the outcome be assessed in a written, oral, or practicum exam or in some kind of assignment? Will the written exam be take-home or in class? Will it revolve around a case study or a real-world problem? Will the specimens be in the lab, in nature, in a photograph, or in a drawing? What media forms will be accepted? Will a revision be allowed? Outcomes may also specify the criteria and standards for the assessment, or at least the quality of acceptable performances, answers, or products. Rubrics do an excellent job of laying out these criteria and standards.

Students have a much better chance of succeeding academically when they know what they are expected to be able to do. Preparing a "test blueprint" clarifies these expectations because it lists the learning outcomes that the test will assess (Suskie, 2004). At least some of these will represent microlevel skills. This blueprint not only ensures a well-conceived exam but also makes the test development process relatively easy for the instructor. For the students, it is a very useful review sheet, much more so than a list of concepts and principles "to know" (Suskie, 2004). It answers their age-old question, "What's going to be on the test?" without giving away the answers to the test questions.

Types of Outcomes

Just about every course has cognitive (thinking) outcomes, but many have other types of outcomes as well: affective (e.g., medical, nursing, public speaking, customer relations, counseling, and education courses), psychomotor (e.g., medical, nursing, veterinary, lab science, public speaking, computer, mechanical, trade, and art courses), or ethical (e.g., medical, nursing, law, and management courses). Courses that include group activities or projects usually have social outcomes, whether faculty make these explicit or not. Because we cannot peer into a person's mind, affective outcomes do not pertain to the internal state of *having* certain emotions, such as compassion, concern, conviction, empathy, and enthusiasm, but to *manifesting* them in observable behavior, such as in a role play, a simulation, or real life. Generally, an expert observer can assess a person's psychomotor skills and sometimes social abilities, although the other members of an interacting group may be in the best position to judge. Finally, ethical outcomes may also be observable in real or simulated situations. More frequently, however, instructors evaluate them by having students analyze and evaluate the ethical ramifications of possible courses of action in a case study.

Fink (2003) proposes a model of six categories of learning that span cognitive, affective, and social outcomes. When incorporated into a course, they together comprise a significant learning experience. Ideally, every course has outcomes in each category that work in tandem to heighten the impact of the learning experience. Fink provides a comprehensive, step-by-step procedure for designing any course using his model, whatever the level, discipline, or delivery mode. The following are his six categories of learning:

1. *Foundational knowledge* is mastering the basic information and fundamental ideas of the field or subfield around which the other types of learning revolve.
2. *Application* is practicing important skills and thinking about the knowledge in practical, critical, and creative ways, all of which make the other kinds of learning useful.
3. *Integration* is making connections among ideas, subfields, disciplines, aspects of one's life, and kinds of learning.
4. *The human dimension* is giving students new insights into themselves, others, and the human implications of other kinds of learning.
5. *Caring* is motivating students to adopt new interests, emotions, attitudes, and/or values related to the material and to want to learn more about it.
6. *Learning how to learn* is adopting self-conscious strategies to learn the material more efficiently and effectively and to learn more generally beyond the course.

Before we move on, a word about cognitive outcomes is in order because they are universal and have generated the most attention in the literature. In fact, they supply most of the examples of outcomes and assignments in this book. Obviously, some thinking processes are more challenging and advanced than others. On the low end are processes such as black-and-white thinking or simply recalling material from a reading or lecture, and on the high end are epistemological reasoning, refined professional judgment, cutting-edge problem solving, the generation of new knowledge, and other sophisticated, expert-level mental operations. Chapter 3 explicates several models for ranking cognitive outcomes from low to high level.

Designing a Course Around Outcomes

The fact that some cognitive processes are more challenging and advanced than others suggests a logical framework for designing a course: Start students out with achieving the lower-level outcomes and lead them up through the higher-level ones. The same applies to affective, psychomotor, ethical, and social outcomes.

Backward design is another process that can help you identify and sequence your learning outcomes. It was developed by Wiggins and McTighe (2005) for elementary and secondary schoolteachers; the basic idea is to begin with the desired learning ends and work backward to identify the necessary means to these ends, including the assessments and instructional strategies. The following description adapts Wiggins and McTighe's model to higher education and updates it with more current approaches to outcomes development and course design.

The first task is to identify the most sophisticated skills and abilities you want your students to acquire. These are presumably the ones that the students will have gained by the *end* of your course. Elsewhere, I call these *ultimate outcomes* (Nilson, 2007, 2010). (The program in which you teach may dictate some of your course's learning outcomes, so check first with your department chair or dean.) Next, you need to consider what outcomes will prepare your students to achieve your ultimate ones—that is, what will the students have to be able to do *before* they can execute the most sophisticated skills and abilities? These are *mediating outcomes*, and you should arrange them in the order in which students can most easily acquire them because some of these outcomes will equip students to tackle other outcomes. In other words, you work your way backward identifying and ordering all the requisite outcomes. The final destinations are the *foundational outcomes*, which are the basic skills and abilities that your students must achieve in the first two to three weeks of the course as preparation to take on the mediating outcomes.

In the end, you will have developed a flowchart of learning outcomes, called an *outcomes map* (Nilson 2007, 2010). It shows the learning process that you will lead your students through, and it complements the text syllabus. After all, the text only lists your outcomes to be achieved by the end of the course, whereas an outcomes map arranges them in the order that your students will work on attaining them. This is the skeleton of your course design, your plan for student learning.

To this skeleton, you will first attach the assessments, the evidence of learning, which is the second stage of Wiggins and McTighe's (2005) backward design schema. We have already covered assessments, so we can advance to the third stage, which involves adding the real "muscle" to the skeleton—that is, planning the learning experiences most appropriate for your outcomes. These student experiences are, in effect, your teaching methods and moves. Methods are assignments and activities that take considerable time and commitment either because they require days or weeks to complete (e.g., long simulations, service-learning experiences, and problem-based learning projects) or because you tend to use them over and over through the term (e.g., interactive lecturing, the case method, discussion, and in-class group exercises). Teaching moves, on the other hand, require only 1 to about 20 minutes. They are brief techniques for making the material clearer, more compelling, more concrete, easier to recall and retrieve, or more relevant, as well as giving students practice working with the material. They encompass not only things you might do (e.g., explain a concept or process in a different way, work a problem for the class, provide examples or applications, concept-map a reading on the board, or model a line of reasoning) but also things you might have your students do individually, in small groups, or as a whole class (e.g., relate new material to what they already know, concept-map a reading, answer a multiple-choice question, develop a multiple-choice question, debrief a case, interpret the data in a table or graph, or detect fallacies in an argument). Given the low time and energy commitment of any one teaching move, you can always try another one if the first one falls flat or needs reinforcement.

Not all teaching methods and moves serve all learning outcomes equally well. Straight lecture alone transfers knowledge but does not develop any skills in students. Just-in-Time Teaching (JiTT) promotes comprehension of new content but rarely high-level cognitive abilities. For advanced thinking skills such as analytic, problem-solving, and evaluative reasoning, the case method and problem-based learning rank among the most effective techniques. As a rule of thumb, the best teaching methods and moves give your students practice in performing the outcomes you have set for them, followed by feedback in how they can perform better. This feedback may come from you, student peers, or teaching assistants. To help students succeed, try to provide at least some opportunities for practice under the same or similar conditions, in the same medium and setting, and with special requirements the same as or similar to those of your graded assessments. So, for example, before you ask students to design a multimedia presentation on a service-learning project, be sure that they have had some practice and feedback on putting together a small multimedia presentation and on reflecting on what they have learned from the project and what they have contributed through it.

Keep in mind that assignments and tests can serve as learning experiences as well as assessments. Having students routinely assess their study/

preparation strategies and conduct error analyses on their graded tests is a very effective learning activity, whatever your outcomes (Achacoso, 2004; Barkley, 2009; Zimmerman, Moylan, Hudesman, White, & Flugman, 2011).

You can find trustworthy advice on selecting the teaching methods and moves that have proven most successful in helping students achieve learning outcomes like yours. Look to the research on college teaching and cognitive processes, as well as your experienced colleagues, to apprise you of your best options. The following books draw on that research to provide recommendations on designing and developing an effective course. Many teaching/faculty development centers also post basic guidelines on their websites.

Biggs, J., & Tang, C. (2011). *Teaching for quality learning at university: What the student does* (4th ed.). Berkshire, England: Open University Press and McGraw-Hill Education.

Blumberg, P. (2009). *Developing learner-centered teaching: A practical guide for faculty.* San Francisco, CA: Jossey-Bass.

Davis, J. R., & Arend, B. D. (2013). *Facilitating seven ways of learning: A resource for more purposeful, effective, and enjoyable college teaching.* Sterling, VA: Stylus.

Fink, L. D. (2003). *Creating significant learning experiences: An integrated approach to designing college courses.* San Francisco, CA: Jossey-Bass.

Fink, L. D., & Fink, A. K. (Eds.). (2009). *Designing courses for significant learning: Voices of experience. New Directions for Teaching and Learning,* No. 119. San Francisco, CA: Jossey-Bass.

Hansen, E. J. (2011). *Idea-based learning: A course design process to promote conceptual understanding.* Sterling, VA: Stylus.

Meyer, J. H. F., & Land, R. (2006). *Overcoming barriers to student understanding: Threshold concepts and troublesome knowledge.* New York, NY: Routledge.

Nilson, L. B. (2007). *The graphic syllabus and the outcomes map: Communicating your course.* San Francisco, CA: Jossey-Bass.

Nilson, L. B. (2010). *Teaching at its best: A research-based resource for college instructors* (3rd ed.). San Francisco, CA: Jossey-Bass.

Prégent, R. (2000). *Charting your course: How to prepare to teach more effectively.* Madison, WI: Atwood.

Richlin, L. (2006). *Blueprint for learning: Creating college courses to facilitate, assess, and document learning.* Sterling, VA: Stylus.

Ritter, F. E., Nerb, J., Lehtinen, E., & O'Shea, T. M. (2007). *In order to learn: How the sequence of topics influences learning.* New York, NY: Oxford University Press.

3

LINKING GRADES TO OUTCOMES

In our current grading system, we grade a student's work by how close it comes to what we want, and what we want is what gets an A. In actuality, only the students who earn an A in a course come close to achieving the outcomes we hope for. A grade of C does not communicate competency in any particular skill or ability; students routinely pass courses even though their graded work falls considerably below our objectives for them. Because we are under enormous pressure to pass students and have a great deal of discretion in evaluating students, grades do not translate into competencies or outcomes. Perhaps this is why public and government agencies are clamoring for accountability, and why assessment agencies ignore grades and seek evidence of student competencies from program-level sources, whether standardized tests or portfolios or something else.

What Course Grades Should Mean

If we structure our courses around students' achieving learning outcomes, shouldn't our students' course grades correspond to the learning outcomes they have achieved? This is what Walvoord and Anderson (2009) recommend, but we generally do not grade this way. Physics professor Andy

Rundquist seems to be one of the few faculty who grade students solely on their outcomes achievement. He gives them multiple chances to achieve his outcomes, and he reassesses his students until they achieve them—or the semester ends. He does not grade on attendance, effort, or anything else (Beatty, 2012). By logical extension, each assignment or test should ask students to demonstrate their achievement of one or more outcomes (Chun, 2010; Fox, 2010). In other words, students should gain credit for showing evidence of achieving learning outcomes. Outcomes achievement is not a matter of degree; a student either achieves an outcome or does not achieve it in any given assessment.

Achieving outcomes is comparable to making it over hurdles in an athletic competition. Therefore, a course grade should reflect the *number* of hurdles the student jumps (i.e., the number of outcomes she achieves) or the *height* of the hurdles she jumps (i.e., the level of cognitive sophistication or complexity she demonstrates) or both. For each hurdle or outcome, an instructor must delineate work requirements that a student product must meet to merit credit. These assessment requirements must show clear evidence of outcomes achievement based on built-in quality standards. One set of work requirements can map onto one or several outcomes.

In operational terms, students receive grades based on the *number* of work requirements and/or the *specific* work requirements they complete at a satisfactory level by given due dates. In other words, students earn higher grades by jumping *more* hurdles that show evidence of *more* learning (i.e., mastery of a greater amount or breadth of knowledge or a greater number of skills on the same level) and/or jumping *higher* hurdles that show evidence of *more advanced* learning, or both. While the idea of more hurdles is a relatively simple matter of quantity of work, the notion of higher hurdles reflects the more complex matter of the greater cognitive sophistication or challenge of the work: correctly solving more complex or more difficult problems or demonstrating higher-order cognitive skills, higher levels of cognitive development, or higher levels of problem-solving thought in a piece of written work. Fortunately, we can examine some cognitive models that can elucidate the meaning of *higher hurdles*.

Defining More Advanced Learning

Several cognition-based frameworks are available for defining levels of learning, from basic through advanced. The following sections discuss these frameworks.

Bloom's Taxonomy of Cognitive Operations

The best known and oldest cognition-based schema is Bloom's (Bloom & Associates, 1956) taxonomy or hierarchy of cognitive operations:

- Knowledge: to memorize or recognize facts and terms
- Comprehension: to translate or restate in one's own words
- Application: to utilize, apply, solve, or make useful
- Analysis: to identify, examine, and come to conclusions about parts or components, such as comparing and contrasting and deducing assumptions and implications
- Synthesis: to make new connections among parts or components, such as identifying relationships or creating something new
- Evaluation: to assess, judge, or defend quality, value, or validity

Bloom posited that the operations become more complex and advanced moving from knowledge to evaluation, and that a learner must be able to master all the lower-order ones before becoming adept at the higher-order ones. For example, to conduct a sound analysis of an argument, students must be able to identify relevant facts, terms, and "knowns" of the subject matter; restate them in their own words; and apply them to a problem or real-world situation. Mastering analysis of the subject opens the door to learning synthesis, and synthesis to evaluation.

Anderson and Krathwohl's Revision of Bloom's Taxonomy

Anderson and Krathwohl (2000) introduced a gerund-based revision of Bloom's taxonomy. It more accurately names the lowest-order cognitive operation, gives synthesis a more imaginative nuance, and reorders the two highest-order cognitive operations:

- Remembering
- Understanding
- Applying
- Analyzing
- Evaluating
- Creating

In Bloom's schema, evaluation is the most advanced type of learning, whereas in this revised version creating is the most advanced. Otherwise, the principle is the same: Demonstrating the higher-order cognitive operations is evidence of more advanced learning.

Perry's Stages of Undergraduate Cognitive Development

Another cognition-based framework that posits a progression from basic to more advanced learning is William G. Perry's (1968) stages of undergraduate cognitive development. Whereas the sequence of cognitive operations in Bloom's and Anderson and Krathwohl's hierarchies is open to debate, Perry's stages follow a hard-and-fast order. They outline the process by which a student comes to understand the true nature of knowledge as inherently uncertain, incomplete human creations but still subject to definite standards of comparison on quality, validity, and utility.

In his short four-stage schema (the longer nine-stage schema only makes fine distinctions within the four stages), Perry called the intellectual perspective of the first stage "dualism." Students first look upon a discipline-based body of knowledge as a large aggregate of information, something like a long list of phone numbers. It is a collection of facts, rules, and vocabulary words to memorize. Further, these facts, rules, and terms are "real"; the facts are indisputable, the rules always apply, and the terms name existing things or phenomena. In other words, you can be absolutely certain of the validity and reality of whatever is in that body of knowledge and, by implication, whatever the textbook says. A statement is either "right," if it is found in that body of knowledge, or "wrong," if some piece of knowledge in that body contradicts it. Moreover, disciplinary experts such as faculty have a ready command of all that knowledge. Their job is to simply regurgitate it in writing, as stated in a textbook or an article, or verbally, as said in a lecture, so the students can "absorb" and memorize as many of the facts, rules, and terms as possible.

No doubt this type of fact-anchored, black-and-white, right-or-wrong thinking is characteristic of most undergraduates and, frankly, most people in general. Students in this stage see little organization to the aggregate of information on a subject and, logically enough, believe that the way to learn it is to memorize it for either recognition or regurgitation on the next test. With this perspective on the nature of knowledge, the only level of thinking is remembering, which is the lowest level in Anderson and Krathwohl's taxonomy.

A student will not progress beyond dualism unless she learns that bodies of knowledge contain uncertainty—that is, they do not cover all there is to know. Gaps in knowledge exist. Some future events are not precisely predictable. Questions remain unanswered. The critical question is, Why? At the second of Perry's stages of undergraduate cognitive development, called "multiplicity," the student thinks that the uncertainty stems from the incompetency of experts to find all the answers, or that the instructor is leading her to believe uncertainty exists for the sake of some kind of intellectual exercise.

But she may soon decide that the unknowns are real but only a temporary problem while experts complete their research to "fill in" the factual blanks.

Reaching the third stage represents a qualitative leap in a student's understanding of the nature of knowledge. It rests on the insight that knowledge is not something that really exists "out there" and is merely waiting to be discovered and named. Rather, knowledge is a *human cognitive creation*—scholars' interpretation of specific observations and data, some apparent patterns and trends that experts have identified, a grid that authorities put over a messy reality to make sense of it. Imperfect as it may be, this grid allows us to predict and manipulate our world to some extent and often to increase our collective survival chances. But at its core, knowledge is *inherently* uncertain.

Perry called this third stage "relativism." Although a fairly advanced stage of thinking, it fails to distinguish degrees of quality among different paradigms or grids. The relativistic learner discredits the most informed, well-grounded interpretations and even knowledge itself as "someone's opinion." As a logical extension of this perspective, each opinion rates about the same, and therefore the student's opinion ranks about as valid as the next. Of course, students usually realize that such thinking does not help in factual matters and that they are unlikely to come up with a theory of their own regarding the physics or chemistry of the universe. However, they may use this reasoning to justify their belief in creationism or intelligent design, individualism (in opposition to social structural explanations of human outcomes), and just about any ethical system. Perhaps corrupt government officials and corporate leaders have rationalized their ethical breaches using a relativistic perspective. In fact, relativism can excuse just about any value, belief, and action that human beings are capable of. For this reason, it can be a dangerous landing for students to rest on very long. In time, the libertarian excitement of relativism may wear off as they find themselves having to qualify its principles and live with too many internal contradictions ("It's okay to cheat someone except when the victim is a child, parent, spouse, minister, friend, pregnant woman, etc."). Should this happen, students will welcome entering the next stage of development.

The fourth and final stage is called "commitment," which means making a tentative commitment to the best available paradigm or grid. Students advance this far upon realizing that not all interpretations are equally valid and useful and that the interpretations of experts are not just their opinions. On a personal level, this insight prompts them to choose a certain viewpoint, ideology, or moral code after examining the strengths and weaknesses of various alternatives. Students view their choice as the best they can make for now and understand its limitations and trade-offs. Perhaps at some time in the future, they will adjust or change their commitment as they acquire greater knowledge and wisdom. On an intellectual level, a student comes to realize, at least for this discipline, that experts compare competing interpretations. They write philosophical treatises arguing the merits and deficits of varying perspectives. They conduct careful scientific research—at crucial junctures, critical experiments—to assess the relative strengths and weaknesses of competing paradigms (Kuhn, 1996). They maintain high, well-developed standards to justify favoring one over another. These may involve scientific evidence, plausibility, precedence, or the safety of human life, depending on the discipline.

Undergraduates do not necessarily progress through these stages of cognitive development. In fact, they may graduate from college with the same dualistic mind-set with which they entered. Faculty may have to consciously help their students advance through the stages. They would do well to set learning outcomes and integrate learning activities with the aim of moving their students through a couple, if not all, of these stages.

Wolcott and Lynch's Thinking Performance Patterns

The final framework that defines *lower-level* through *higher-level learning* was developed by Wolcott and Lynch (2006a; Wolcott, 2006). It is built on a hierarchy of four problem-solving skills that vary by level of complexity (Wolcott, 2006). The least complex (step 1) is identifying, which involves pointing out and describing the relevant information as well as the uncertainties (risks) and unknowns. Step 2 is exploring, which entails interpreting information from different standpoints and organizing it into categories. In Bloom's or Anderson and Krathwohl's hierarchies, this level of thinking would be quite high, overlapping with analysis (of advantages and disadvantages), synthesis/creating (categories), and even evaluation (of the information). But in Wolcott and Lynch's, it is quite basic. Step 3 is prioritizing, which includes drawing and assessing sound conclusions, appraising risk, developing plans and policies, and implementing them with the participation of others. Anderson and Krathwohl's concepts of evaluating and creating are reflected here, but so are leadership and communication. The final step is re-visioning, which combines analyzing the limitations of a problem-solving strategy, charting future directions and strategies, monitoring and evaluating these strategies, and adjusting them as needed. Again, evaluating, creating, and leading are the major challenges, but unlike in the prioritizing step, they are forward looking.

These four steps provide the foundation for Wolcott and Lynch's (2006a) five Thinking Performance Patterns. Ascending a hierarchy, the patterns demonstrate more complex and sophisticated thinking skills represented by the steps described in Table 3.1.

TABLE 3.1.

Steps for Better Thinking Performance Patterns

← Less Complex Performance Patterns			More Complex Performance Patterns →	
"Confused Fact-Finder" Performance Pattern 0 *Step 1, 2, 3, & 4 skills weak*	*"Biased Jumper"* Performance Pattern 1 *Step 2, 3, & 4 skills weak*	*"Perpetual Analyzer"* Performance Pattern 2 *Step 3 & 4 skills weak*	*"Pragmatic Performer"* Performance Pattern 3 *Step 4 skills weak*	*"Strategic Re-Visioner"* Performance Pattern 4 *Strategically integrates step 1, 2, & 3 skills*
Overall Problem Approach:	**Overall Problem Approach:**	**Overall Problem Approach:**	**Overall Problem Approach:**	**Overall Problem Approach:**
Proceeds as if goal is to find the single "correct" answer	Proceeds as if goal is to stack up evidence and information to support conclusion	Proceeds as if goal is to establish a detached, balanced view of evidence and information from different points of view	Proceeds as if goal is to come to a well-founded conclusion based on objective comparisons of viable alternatives	Proceeds as if goal is to construct knowledge, to move toward better conclusions or greater confidence in conclusions as the problem is addressed over time
Common Weaknesses:	**Major Improvements Over Performance Pattern 0:**	**Major Improvements Over Performance Pattern 1:**	**Major Improvements Over Performance Pattern 2:**	**Major Improvements Over Performance Pattern 3:**
• Fails to realistically perceive uncertainties/ ambiguities • Does not seem to "get it"; recasts open-ended problem to one having a single "correct" answer	• Acknowledges existence of enduring uncertainties and the viability of multiple perspectives • Begins to use evidence logically to support conclusions	• Presents coherent and balanced description of a problem and its larger context • Identifies issues, assumptions, and biases associated with multiple perspectives	• After thorough exploration, consciously prioritizes issues and information	• Prioritizes and addresses limitations effectively

	Common Weaknesses:		Common Weaknesses:	Common Weaknesses:
• Insists that professors, textbooks, or other experts should provide "correct" answer • Expresses confusion or futility • Uses illogical/contradictory arguments • Cannot evaluate or appropriately apply evidence • Inappropriately cites textbook, "facts," or definitions • Conclusion based on unexamined authorities' views or what "feels right"	• Jumps to conclusions • Stacks up evidence quantitatively to support own view and ignores contrary information • Equates unsupported personal opinion with other forms of evidence • Inept at breaking problem down and understanding multiple perspectives • Insists that all opinions are equally valid, but ignores or discounts other opinions • Views experts as being opinionated or as trying to subject others to their personal beliefs	• Attempts to control own biases • Logically and qualitatively evaluates evidence from different viewpoints **Common Weaknesses:** • Unable to establish priorities for judging across alternatives • Reluctant to select and defend a single overall solution as most viable, or provides inadequate support for solution • Writes overly long paper in an attempt to demonstrate all aspects of analysis (problems without prioritizing) • Jeopardizes class discussions by getting stuck on issues such as definitions	• Articulates well-founded support for choosing one solution while objectively considering other viable options • Conclusion based on qualitative evaluation of experts' positions or situational pragmatics • Effectively incorporates others in the decision process and/or implementation **Common Weaknesses:** • Conclusion doesn't give sufficient attention to long-term, strategic issues • Inadequately identifies and addresses solution limitations and "next steps"	• Interprets and re-interprets bodies of information systematically over time as new information becomes available • Exhibits a strategic, long-term vision • Spontaneously considers possible ways to generate new information about the problem **Common Weaknesses:** • Not applicable

The simplest pattern is that of the Confused Fact-Finder, which has mastered none of the skills of the four steps. Paralleling dualism, this mind-set defines *problem solving* as a quest to find the one correct solution or answer.

Next is the Biased Jumper, which "jumps" to a problem solution without assessing all the data or entertaining alternatives. This type of mind is proficient only in identifying relevant information, which is characteristic of step 1. So it views problem solving as amassing evidence to support its hastily chosen solution. Like Perry's relativistic thinker, the mentality of the Biased Jumper considers all opinions as equally valid but discounts those different from its own. In addition, it sees authorities as trying to force their opinions on others.

Third up the hierarchy lies the Perpetual Analyzer, a mind-set strong in identifying and exploring information (step 2) but weak in the skills of steps 3 and 4. It strives to reach an objective, balanced view of the evidence and represent every approach to the problem. However, it lacks the standards to prioritize and decide among the perspectives available, making informed judgment and committed action impossible. While more sophisticated than the Biased Jumper, the Perpetual Analyzer is also relativistic in regarding all opinions as equally valid, but the latter discounts none of them. In Perry's framework, this is the advanced stage of relativism. The paralysis it engenders readies a person to seek commitment.

The fourth approach to problem solving is represented by the Pragmatic Performer, which is proficient in the skills of steps 1–3. With no problem prioritizing, this mind-set aims to arrive at and implement the most strongly supported conclusion after rationally comparing the various alternatives. It may study expert opinions on the matter and solicit the advice of other involved parties. While prepared to make a commitment to the best available approach, the Pragmatic Performer prefers certainty over tentativeness and may miss some of the limitations and longer term ramifications of the selected decision—in other words, it comes to premature closure and resists contrary evidence and change.

Only the Strategic Re-Visioner brings the thinking skills of all four steps to developing a problem solution. While avoiding closure, this mentality takes action guided by long-term strategic goals. The tentativeness of its commitment to a course of action motivates a continual reassessment of prior decisions and, therefore, ongoing collection and analysis of additional information over time. Because the Strategic Re-Visioner is not emotionally attached to or ego involved with a solution, this mind-set is ever sensitive to the limitations of its chosen strategies and conclusions and is open to adjusting them as conditions change, new information appears, or better alternatives emerge.

Obviously, progressing through the problem-solving skills from steps 1 through 4 and ascending the hierarchy of Thinking Performance Patterns from the Confused Fact-Finder through the Strategic Re-Visioner demonstrates the acquisition of more complex, advanced thinking. When confronted with a fuzzy problem, the student who displays more thinking skills and a higher-level performance pattern in developing a solution is jumping higher hurdles than one who manifests fewer skills and a lower-level performance pattern.

Mathematical and Logical Problems

Anyone who has ever taken a course in mathematics, physics, or computer science knows that the end-of-chapter problems start out with some straightforward drill-type problems that look like those that the chapter used for demonstration. Students can solve these with a plug-and-chug strategy that requires little or no quantitative reasoning or understanding of the concepts and principles involved. As the problems progress, they become more difficult. Perhaps the contexts of the word problems morph in unanticipated ways. Or the problems contain an unexpected unknown. Or they look like a problem from an earlier lesson that required a different algorithm to solve. Or the solutions entail multiple steps. Or they require not just the chapter's lesson but an integration of materials from previous chapters as well. Or visualizing the parts of the problems is essential to determining the right approach. Any number of factors can make problems more challenging.

For whatever reasons, fewer students are able to solve more complex problems, and those who do usually take longer to solve them than the easier problems. Solving such problems, and doing so within a reasonable time frame, demonstrates more advanced thinking than solving only the easier textbook problems.

Summary of the Frameworks

We have reviewed four cognition-based frameworks, one with hierarchies of both problem-solving skills and Thinking Performance Patterns, that define levels of learning from basic through advanced. We have also acknowledged the varying difficulty levels of mathematical and logic-based problems. These different schema for defining levels of learning show that there are various types of advanced learning and many ways to conceive and structure higher hurdles in assignments and test questions.

As Figure 3.1 displays, the height of the hurdles varies independently of the number of hurdles, which is a function of the amount of content

Figure 3.1.   Graphic Representation of Relationship Between More Hurdles and Higher Hurdles

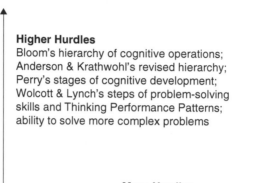

or the number of skills. In any given course, grades may depend solely on quantity—how much content or how many skills students can demonstrate that they have mastered—or on the quality of thinking that students can demonstrate working with the content, or on a combination of quantity and quality. The fact that the frameworks we have examined define each level of learning so clearly should make the process of laying out work requirements less mysterious.

Tying Outcomes Achievement to Grades

It is easy to link students' grades to the learning outcomes they achieve. Each set of work requirements laid out by the instructor should provide evidence that a student has achieved one or more outcomes. Therefore, grades should reflect the number of outcomes achieved at a satisfactory level (e.g., achieving all 10 outcomes earns an A, achieving nine earns a B, eight earns a C, etc.), the cognitive level at which outcomes are achieved, or both. If some outcomes are required, an instructor can designate these as essential to pass and others as electives for a higher grade, giving students some choice about the outcomes they will tackle.

The following is a hypothetical grading structure that explains each course grade in terms of the outcomes that students will achieve by fulfilling the given work requirements:

- For a D: Pass two midterms and the final, with a total average score of at least 70%. The work required to meet this condition will give you minimal mastery of most of the course material.
- For a C: All that is required for a D, plus turn in a one-page, typewritten outline of each reading assignment on the day it is due (single-spaced, standard margins, 12-point type). Each outline will be considered acceptable if it fulfills the length and formatting requirements, shows a good-faith effort, and does not resemble anyone else's. Two late *or* unacceptable submissions (only two) are allowed for any reason. (Exceeding two exceptions automatically drops your course grade to a D.) This additional series of assignments will help ensure that you read all the assigned reading material thoroughly and leave the course with a decent mastery of it.
- For a B: All that is required for a C, plus write four reflection papers, each typewritten 500–700 words and turned in on time, on your progress made in mastering the material. Be sure to analyze these factors: what study, note-taking, reading, and other learning methods you have been using; your areas of strength and comfort as a result; your remaining areas of confusion, difficulty, and/or discomfort; and what else you plan to do to master especially challenging material. This additional series of writing assignments will help ensure that you reflect on the course material and the process of your learning it, thereby helping to ensure you leave the course with a good mastery of both the course material and how you best learn it so you can pursue the subject matter efficiently in the future.
- For an A: All that is required for a B, plus you will be placed on a team with other students pursuing an A to solve a major real-world problem using the course material. This learning experience is called problem-based learning. You will have to identify unknowns and conduct research beyond the course material to develop a sound solution. The problem will be fuzzy in that it will have more than one possible approach and solution, but some will be better than others. This additional assignment will help ensure not only that you will have mastered the course material, but also that you can apply it, research additional related material, and synthesize it all to solve a genuine problem facing the world today. [Instructors might consider other possible A-level assignments that are also authentic and creative, such as a policy statement; a strategic plan; persuasive memos; a newspaper, magazine, or journal article; a business plan; or a mind map or concept map of a subject or the field displaying its organization and issues.]

Let's now venture beyond the hypothetical and examine the grading structures of real courses based on more hurdles, higher hurdles, and a combination of both.

Grading on More Hurdles

In this section, we look at two examples of courses designed and taught by Kathleen Kegley (personal communication, January 5, 2009), who has both a botany and a management background. Each example illustrates a simple and slightly different grading structure. Chapter 6 explains the terms *modules* and *bundles* in detail, so for now just a simple definition will suffice: Both are collections of assessments; however, modules are sequenced whereas bundles are not.

Kegley structures her Plant Medicine course around fact-based material. The learning outcomes focus on recognizing, memorizing, and applying basic terminology and concepts and categorizing plants, plant pathologies, and treatment strategies, and her course modules reflect these outcomes. Her students earn a C in the course for having an average score of 70% or higher across the exams, all of which are objective. These assess students' abilities to recognize, recall, and apply basic terminology and concepts and grossly classify plants, plant pathologies, and treatment strategies. For a B, students have to meet the requirement for a C and complete sets of assignments that go into more detail on six different plants. Correspondingly, the classification schemes become finer. For an A, students must meet the requirements for a B *and* complete sets of assignments on six *more* plants, for a total of 12 plants. In other words, students have to master more content to attain a higher grade, but the cognitive sophistication demanded is about the same for each grade. This course illustrates a very simple, user-friendly grading structure:

- Successfully complete Module 1 to get a C.
- Successfully complete Modules 1 and 2 to get a B.
- Successfully complete Modules 1, 2, and 3 to get an A.

Following a slightly more complex structure, Kegley designed her advanced undergraduate course, Management Information Systems, around five bundles. Each bundle contains multiple activities that vary in difficulty from straight knowledge and comprehension to creative problem solving and self-assessment. Therefore, each one offers and assesses the same level of cognitive challenge and sophistication. Course grades reflect the number of bundles successfully completed:

- To receive an A in the course, students must successfully complete all five *Basic Learning Bundles* plus the corresponding *"A" Track* (Kegley's terms) assignments by the stated deadlines.
- To receive a B in the course, students must successfully complete all five Basic Learning Bundles by the stated deadlines.
- To receive a C in the course, students must successfully complete any four of the Basic Learning Bundles by the stated deadlines.
- To receive a D in the course, students must successfully complete any three of the Basic Learning Bundles by the stated deadlines.
- Failure to complete the requirements for a D will result in an F in the course.

However, each bundle addresses a different topic. So Kegley makes it very clear that only students who successfully complete all five Basic Learning Bundles will be able to achieve all of the five following outcomes:

1. Intelligently discuss issues related to Information, Information Technology, and MIS professionals.
2. Explain computerized decision support, analysis, and design tools.
3. Explain the role technology plays in decision-making processes.
4. Explain managerial issues involved in MIS, such as design, implementation, technology, and system usage.
5. Develop and apply creative thinking skills as applied to using computers in business.

An additional outcome is available only to students completing the "A" Track projects:

6. Develop your own personal strategies for mastering new software packages that are related to your career goals.

Grading on Higher Hurdles

A particularly simple and transparent example of grading students purely on jumping higher hurdles was developed by computer science professor Dr. Laurence L. Leff. He published his grading system on the web, calling it "Assignment Set Based Contract Grading" (Leff, n.d.). It rests on the idea that some programming tasks are more challenging than others—that is, they diverge further from the template problems and solution strategies that the text and the instructor provide in the teaching process. Leff designed a range of assignments of varying difficulty for each major course topic. Completing only the easiest ones—let's say six assignments—earns students a C, doing the intermediate set of six earns them a B, and completing the most difficult set of six earns them an A. Good-faith attempts that do not yield a valid solution—in this case, a workable program that accomplishes the specified task—do not count. Note that students complete the same number of assignments no matter which grade they are aiming for. Those who want an A do not carry a heavier workload, although the more challenging assignments may take more time. Presumably, students who can complete assignments at a higher level can easily do all of those at lower levels, so there is no reason to make them perform the lower-level tasks. This grading structure would transfer well to mathematics and most other problem-solving disciplines.

Leff adds an interesting wrinkle to his system, building in an incentive for students to submit all their assignments on time. He requires the smallest number of assignments if the students hand them in on time, a few more assignments if they turn them in slightly late, and still more if they hand them in very late. You may want to superimpose this temporal layer on your grading system.

To grade on higher hurdles without adding hurdles for the higher grades requires clear-cut levels of difficulty among the assignments. More challenging assignments must incorporate the skills of more basic ones or transcend them. Both Bloom's and Anderson and Krathwohl's hierarchies of cognitive operations are built on the premise that a learner must have mastered all lower-order types of thinking before he can perform the next higher type. So, for example, he cannot analyze material before he can remember, understand, and apply it. In other words, thinking skills are *cumulative*. Wolcott and Lynch's hierarchy of problem-solving skills is similarly cumulative. A student who can acknowledge the limitations of his information (step 4) can surely identify what information is relevant (step 1). However, Perry's stages of undergraduate cognitive development and Wolcott and Lynch's hierarchy of Thinking Performance Patterns operate quite differently. The higher levels of thinking *replace* and *transcend* those of levels beneath them. A developing mind is "growing up" through the steps, advancing beyond the errors and limitations of the previous steps.

Wolcott and Lynch (2006b) make it easy to see how their hierarchy of problem-solving skills and Thinking Performance Patterns may support a grading system based on jumping higher hurdles. They developed lists of assignment questions to match the defining skills at the various problem-solving skill steps, shown in the template in Table 3.2. Students who can perform the tasks listed in any given column have attained the thinking skills that label that column. They have moved beyond the more limited thinking of previous steps and have acquired new, more sophisticated skills. You can design a substantial written assignment that asks students to perform various tasks characteristic of each step. Or you can set up a lengthy simulation that incorporates opportunities to perform tasks at different levels. Then you grade your students' work according to the most advanced step at which they can perform the tasks—for example, a D for performing only at step 1, a C for performing at step 2 but no higher, a B for performing at step 3 but no higher, and an A for performing at step 4. You can also grade according to Wolcott and Lynch's Thinking Performance Patterns, but struggling students may take offense to being called a "Confused Fact-Finder."

Note that students will not wind up achieving the same learning outcomes at the end of the course unless they all aspire to and earn the same grade. This fact may present problems in courses for which the curriculum or an accrediting agency prescribes learning outcomes. In such cases, achieving those learning outcomes should be required to earn a baseline C in the course. Then students receiving a B or an A will have exceeded achieving the prescribed outcomes.

Grading on Both More and Higher Hurdles

Setting up a grading system that rewards both additional work and more advanced work implies that the additional work will be more advanced. Recall that students graded according to their performance on Wolcott and Lynch's (2006b) hierarchy of problem solving skills and Thinking Performance Patterns would not have to do additional work for higher grades; their work would just have to demonstrate more advanced learning. Also recall that not all students are likely to achieve the same outcomes. This is the case with grading on both more and higher hurdles. Therefore, any required learning outcomes in a course following this grading schema should determine the standards for the C.

Let's draw on Bloom's hierarchy of cognitive operations to develop a hypothetical illustration of grading on both more and higher hurdles:

- For a D (or an F) in the course, fail to meet the minimal requirements for a C, which demand only basic knowledge and comprehension of 70% of the material.

TABLE 3.2.
Template for Designing Assignment Questions

← Less Complex Skills		More Complex Skills →	
Step 1—Identifying	*Step 2—Exploring*	*Step 3—Prioritizing*	*Step 4—Re-Visioning*
Identifying Relevant Information	**Interpreting Information From Multiple Viewpoints**	**Prioritizing and Concluding**	**Acknowledging Limitations**
• List data or types of information relevant to ____.	• Describe the pros and cons (or advantages/ disadvantages, or strengths/ weaknesses) of ____.	• Develop and use reasonable guidelines for drawing conclusions regarding ____.	• Identify and describe potential future developments in ____.
• Identify relevant information in (a textual passage such as a case, an article, or a piece of literature).	• Analyze the costs and benefits of ____.	• Assess the amount of uncertainty (or degree of risk) of ____.	• Describe limitations to a recommendation about ____.
• Identify or access relevant theories, laws, standards, or rules for ____.	• Explain how ambiguities affect your analysis of ____.	• Objectively consider ____ when making a decision about ____.	• Strategically/proactively consider contingencies and future developments related to ____.
• Identify factors or issues related to ____.	• Identify assumptions associated with (a point of view or alternative) ____.	• Prioritize ____.	
• Identify various potential points of view or solutions to ____.	• Interpret ____ from the viewpoint of ____.	• Consider ____ in reaching a conclusion.	**Creating and Monitoring Strategies**
• Describe arguments in favor of ____.	• Appropriately use (a technique) to analyze ____.	• Develop reasonable recommendation(s) for ____.	• Develop and monitor strategies for ____.
	• Objectively evaluate ____ information.	• Address the costs and benefits of ____ in reaching a conclusion about ____.	• Implement appropriate corrective action for ____ over time.
		• Develop reasonable policies for ____.	

Identifying Uncertainties

- Describe uncertainties concerning _____.
- Identify and describe uncertainties about the interpretation or significance of _____.
- Identify risks associated with _____.
- Describe why there is no single "correct" way to _____.
- Identify reasons why _____ might change or vary.

- Explain how alternative solutions might affect _____ (one or more individuals, organizations, groups, or other stakeholders).
- Analyze the quality of information and evidence related to _____.
- Identify own biases and explain how those biases were controlled when _____.
- Identify the effects of _____ on _____.

Organizing Information

- Develop meaningful categories for analyzing information about _____.
- Organize the various aspects of _____ to assist in decision making.

- Develop an effective plan for addressing _____.

Effectively Involving Others in Implementation

- Take actions to implement the best solution to _____.
- Organize (a communication) so that it is meaningful to the receiving party.
- Communicate effectively for (a given setting and audience).

- Acknowledge changing circumstances and reconsider (a solution) as appropriate.
- Continuously monitor and update _____, as needed.
- Develop strategic uses of _____.
- Manage _____ under changing or unusual demands.
- Apply continuous improvement principles to _____.

Reprinted with permission from Wolcott, S. K., & Lynch, C. L. (2006, February 9). Template for Designing Assignment Questions. Available at www.wolcottlynch.com/Downloadable_Files/Assignment%20Templates_060209.pdf.

- For a C in the course, earn a total of 70% or higher on multiple-choice exams that test basic knowledge and comprehension of the material.
- For a B in the course, fulfill all the requirements for a C, plus successfully complete additional work that demonstrates application and analysis—for example, solving problems that require choices among different possible approaches or algorithms or writing a paper on how a real-life situation or event exemplifies a certain concept or phenomenon.
- For an A in the course, fulfill all the requirements for a B, plus successfully complete additional work that demonstrates synthesis and evaluation—for example, writing a paper that integrates course material and outside research to develop several solutions to a fuzzy problem and appraising each alternative for its strengths and weaknesses.

Now let's look at some real examples of courses that follow this grading system. The first illustration, which roughly follows Bloom's hierarchy, comes from Dr. Wayne Stewart's undergraduate course, International Business Management (personal communication, November 7, 2011). He sets a grade of C as a baseline, informing students that not meeting the requirement for a C will result in a D as long as their point total exceeds 300; otherwise, they will receive an F. The work requirements for a C assess the outcomes of being able to use the concepts and explain the practices involved in managing a company with multinational operations. To get a B or an A entails successfully completing additional and more challenging work. A grade of B requires and assesses students' ability to distill and summarize the most important points in business articles and to analyze their business implications. An A further requires and assesses the sophisticated ability to conduct a high-quality foreign market analysis, synthesis, and assessment, as well as present (teach) it to the class.

- Requirements for a grade of C:
  1. Earn a minimum of 350 out of a potential total of 500 points from exams (400 possible points from three in-class exams and one final) and from other learning activities (100 possible points).
- Requirements for a grade of B: In addition to those for a C:
  1. Do not have more than four unexcused absences, including those associated with being tardy for class (two tardies constitute an absence).

2. Read and submit on time *acceptable* (defined as meeting the criteria stated below and deemed as above average caliber) reviews of five special issues from *The Economist*. You should (1) summarize the essential points of the articles associated with the special issue and (2) provide your reaction to those essential points, including a thorough and thoughtful assessment of the implications for doing business, particularly as related to concepts and discussions from the class.

- Requirements for a grade of A: In addition to those for a B:

    1. Alone or with one other student, conduct and submit on time an *acceptable* (defined as meeting all of the criteria explained later and deemed as A caliber) foreign market assessment, and present it to the class.

Another course incorporating this combination grading system is Design and Implementation of Programming Languages, developed and taught by computer science professor Dr. D. E. ("Steve") Stevenson (personal communication, November 11, 2011). Each ascending grade requires achieving an additional outcome, as assessed by an assignment graded pass/fail, and students must successfully pass each of the earlier milestones to proceed to the next. To pass his course with a C, students must complete a major programming assignment, called a "milestone," that implements local variables and scoping. Each additional milestone is somewhat more advanced. To get a B, students must successfully complete another milestone incorporating non-recursive function calls. And to get an A, they must pass a third milestone demonstrating general recursion.

Our third example is Kegley's online, graduate-level Bioinformatics course, structured around 10 modules (personal communication, January 5, 2009). Each of the first nine focuses on a different textbook chapter (body of content) within the field and assesses the same lower-order outcomes of remembering, understanding, and applying. The tenth, however, entails a hands-on, higher-order cognitive project in which students have to research an open issue in bioinformatics. The learning outcomes for this project encompass analyzing, evaluating, and creating. Students earn a C in the course for completing the first six of the 10 modules at a satisfactory level, a B for completing the first eight at a satisfactory level, and an A for completing all 10 at a satisfactory level. Any student who does not complete the first six modules at a satisfactory level receives an F in the course, but no one ever has. The due dates for the 10 modules are spread out during the semester, which may induce more students to aim for a higher grade than they would if all the modules were due at the same time.

A fourth illustration is chemistry professor Dr. Jeffrey Appling's Scientific Skepticism course, a general-education course integrating the physical, biological, and social sciences. Note how the grading system, depicted in Table 3.3, integrates quantity of work—more assignments and exam questions for higher grades—with the greater challenge of producing more demanding papers and possibly an open-ended creative project, required for an A (personal communication, November 4, 2011).

For a final example of a combination grading system, we can examine one of psychology professor Dr. June J. Pilcher's courses, Advanced Physiological Psychology (personal communication, May 3, 2008). In addition to doing more work for higher grades, students must do more

TABLE 3.3.
Course and Grading Requirements in the Scientific Skepticism Course Taught by Dr. Jeffrey Appling

	Earn C	*Earn B*	*Earn A*
Class Participation (includes no more than three absences, plus group and class discussion and class preparation)	✓	✓	✓
Skeptic Profile	✓	✓	✓
Baloney Detection Kit	✓	✓	✓
Case Study Papers (standards below)	2	3	3
Student Case Study and Reflection Paper (standards below)	✓	✓	✓
Exam 1 (2 questions)			
Exam 2 (2 questions)	4	6	8
Final Exam (4 questions)			
Creative Project (to be arranged with Dr. Appling)		optional*	✓

*Can replace one Case Study Paper or two exam questions.

C papers: 600–1,200 words, modest depth: answer the question using what you learn in class and book; two additional resources cited (Internet okay).

B papers: 1,000–1,500 words, C-level plus more depth: additional resources (two non-Internet), related opinions, and personal reflection.

A papers: >1,250 words, B-level plus *evidence* relating the impact of the topic on society.

sophisticated work. For a C or above, they have to teach two chapters of the textbook, which requires stronger mastery of the material and more advanced learning than does just reading the chapter, writing a summary of it, or answering typical test questions on it. For a B or an A, students must additionally complete a final project that demands creativity, a very high-order cognitive process, either alone or within a team. Pilcher determines whether students will get an A or a B based on the quality of the product.

- Grade of A:
    - Complete and hand in 12 out of 14 possible learning logs by the due date.
    - Read and hand in summaries on 11 out of 12 possible reading assignments by the due date. Note that each reading assignment consists of two to three chapters to read and summarize.
    - Prepare and teach two chapters of your choice.
    - Complete a final project of high quality.
- Grade of B:
    - Complete and hand in 11 out of 14 possible learning logs by the due date.
    - Read and hand in summaries on 10 out of 12 possible reading assignments by the due date. Note that each reading assignment consists of two to three chapters to read and summarize.
    - Prepare and teach two chapters of your choice.
    - Complete a final project of acceptable quality.
- Grade of C:
    - Complete and hand in 10 out of 14 possible learning logs by the due date.
    - Read and hand in summaries on nine out of 12 possible reading assignments by the due date. Note that each reading assignment consists of two to three chapters to read and summarize.
    - Prepare and teach two chapters of your choice.
- Grade of D:
    - Complete and hand in nine out of 14 possible learning logs by the due date.
    - Read and hand in summaries on eight out of 12 possible reading assignments by the due date. Note that each reading assignment consists of two to three chapters to read and summarize.

- Grade of F:
  - ○ Complete and hand in fewer than nine out of 14 possible learning logs.
  - ○ Read and summarize fewer than eight out of 12 possible reading assignments.

The outcome of the final project is for students to explain how and why some aspect of human brain behavior impacts outward behavior. While this task involves outside research, the product could be merely descriptive. But students must exercise creativity in communicating their explanation in a novel modality, such as a half-hour video documentary, a series of public-service TV commercials, a set of informational brochures, or a research proposal requesting funding. Options for a team project could include staging a well-documented debate or an educational play of about a half hour.

Making Grades Meaningful

All the components of a cohesively designed course go back to learning outcomes: homework, class activities, major assignments, tests, and your teaching methods and moves. Why should grades stand apart from outcomes? As these many, varied examples of courses have shown, linking course grades to learning outcomes achieved is a simple and straightforward process. The perhaps unsettling aspect of the link is how we should grade our assessments of our students if they are to reflect outcomes achievement. If students either demonstrate achievement of an outcome or not, must we grade our assessments pass/fail? We will address this question in chapter 4 and begin to develop a new grading system in chapter 5.

4

PASS/FAIL GRADING FOR RIGOR, MOTIVATION, AND FACULTY PEACE OF MIND

If you are like most faculty, you are sometimes unhappy with the quality of the work your students hand in, and you know they could do better if they just made the effort and took the time. Often enough to raise concern, they do not follow directions, answer the question, or complete the problems or writing task. Other times they do a shallow job, spending only minutes the previous night or just before class whipping out an assignment that should have taken them at least one or two hours. It seems they are not trying very hard.

But why should they? We will accept the work to grade and will look for things to give them points for: starting the problem solution off right, even if the solution strategy goes awry or derails because of a careless error; mentioning the correct concepts, even if the words between the concepts make little sense; or giving enough information in a response to suggest some understanding of the material, even if the question we asked is ignored. Of course, we want our students to do well, but should we give them credit and points when they are not doing well as a result of their own carelessness, laziness, or lack of motivation? We cannot expect them to do everything we ask them to do right the first time, but shouldn't we be able to expect them to read and follow the directions, persevere when perplexed, finish the entire assignment, and check or edit their answers?

If we are going to give partial credit for substandard work, then no, we cannot expect students to meet these simple requirements. What is the incentive? Are a few more points enough motivation to work harder if doing a minimal job will obtain the points they need to get the grade they want? Partial credit has a serious flaw in that it rewards poor work, especially when we are trying to eke out as many points as possible for our students.

Partial credit goes back many decades, but the trend toward lowering the stakes of any given assessment is relatively new. In the 1960s–1980s, a course grade generally rested on two high-stakes exams (a midterm and a final) and usually a term paper or a series of lab reports. Writing-focused courses might require a few high-stakes literature papers. More recently, higher education has moved toward an array of many assessments: weekly or even daily quizzes in addition to multiple midterms and a final exam; multiple short writing assignments, some requiring a revision; weekly journals; in-class worksheets; homework problems; lab reports; group papers or projects with presentations; class or online participation; and attendance. More assessments increase the validity and reliability of the final grade.

This trend has had far-reaching consequences, both positive and negative. As classes have grown in size, faculty grading time has substantially increased and grade tracking has moved online. In turn, many instructors have relied more and more on textbook publisher–produced multiple-choice items for quizzes and exams to keep their grading demands manageable. But so much reliance on objective tests may compromise the quality of student assessment. For students, more grading opportunities reduce the anxiety associated with any one assignment, quiz, or exam because it counts less, sometimes very little, toward the final grade. These multiple chances give poorly prepared students the practice they need in performing academic tasks. However, this trend also reduces the seriousness of any one assessment. It does not matter that much if a student fails to grasp a concept, does not finish the assigned reading, gives up quickly on solving a problem, turns in an incomplete lab report, submits a poorly written first draft, or skips a few journal entries. Besides, the student can expect just about anything she turns in to get *some* points. Perhaps our well-intended efforts to lower student stress have dampened some students' motivation to persevere, dig deeper, ask for help, and do their best. As a result, more assessments do not necessarily increase the validity and reliability of the final grade.

What if we graded some or all assignments, quizzes, and exams on a pass/fail basis? This would set a bottom line for acceptable—that is, creditworthy—student work, raising the standards for students' performance. It would also *very moderately* raise the stakes for any given work in that a substandard product would receive no credit at all. In fact, Bowen (2012) argues that students learn best under the conditions of high standards and low stakes, where low stakes may take the form of a supportive learning environment and a caring, encouraging instructor. Might a system of pass/fail grading of assignments and tests supply the motivation for students to follow the directions, finish an assignment, work harder, and produce higher quality work?

What We Know About Pass/Fail Grading

We examine three different contexts in which pass/fail grading has been used: the course, the program, and assignments and tests within a course.

Pass/Fail Grading of Courses: An Ambiguous History

Many faculty are acquainted with the concept of pass/fail as applied to *courses*. The University of Michigan introduced the practice in 1850, and a more modern version of it emerged and gained limited popularity in the 1960s and early 1970s. Typically, the pass level was set at C or C- and students could opt to take a course pass/fail under certain conditions. For example, the course could not be in the student's major, or only one pass/fail course was allowed per term. Despite the restrictions, pass/fail grading earned a mixed reputation. Let's first review the four decades of research on the effects of pass/fail grading on academic standards and student achievement, motivation, satisfaction, and stress.

Most studies from the 1960s and early 1970s found that, compared to traditional letter grading, pass/fail grading of courses lowered academic standards, student motivation, and student achievement (Gatta, 1973; Stallings & Smock, 1971; von Wittich, 1972). Too many students did only enough work to pass the course. Even Princeton undergraduates admitted that they thought they learned more in the traditional grading system than in the pass/fail alternative, and they in fact did perform better on assessments (Karlins, Kaplan, & Stuart, 1969). The one notable exception without negative impacts was a small-scale program involving mainly seniors who were allowed to take non-major courses pass/fail at Virginia Tech (Delohery & McLaughlin, 1971). But on the whole, pass/fail grading of courses seemed to undercut students' motivation to learn and excel and, therefore, lowered academic standards in at least the undergraduate context. By extrapolation, it probably did not foster the development of higher-order cognitive skills either.

Later research conducted on medical students, however, uncovered some important benefits of pass/fail grading. In one study, switching from the letter grade to the pass/fail system reduced the students' stress, fostered student group cohesion, and enhanced students' psychological state of mind

(Rohe, Barrier, & Clark, 2006). In the first year of another pass/fail grading experiment, student performance and satisfaction with the program actually improved (Robins et al., 1995). In another study, first-year residents scored just as high on their clinical performance under the pass/fail system as under letter grading (Vosti & Jacobs, 1999). However, earlier research on medical students and residents yielded mixed results overall (Lloyd, 1992). Still, might maturity make a difference?

Recent research conducted on undergraduate students in Sweden (Dahlgren, Fejes, Abrandt-Dahlgren, & Trowald, 2009) suggests that maturity is not the explanation. In Sweden, some programs—what we would call "majors" with preliminary courses—assess course performance pass/fail and others on a five-level grading scale similar to A–F. This study, involving 402 students at eight universities and university colleges in various professional and liberal arts programs, found that those in the pass/fail category were more than twice as likely to believe that their assessments addressed important aspects of the course than those in the five-level grading system. The latter group was twice as likely to report that they were graded primarily on their ability to recall factual knowledge. Furthermore, three fourths of the pass/fail group viewed their assessments as learning opportunities, whereas less than one third of the five-level grading group did. In other words, pass/fail grading fostered a learning orientation, one motivated by intrinsic rewards, whereas traditional grading encouraged a performance orientation based on extrinsic rewards. The students' differing perceptions and attitudes may not only reflect the grading systems themselves but also how faculty responded to and designed assessments within each system.

It is difficult to draw unambiguous conclusions about the effects of pass/fail grading on academic standards and students. We can say with some confidence that it reduces grading anxiety. But with respect to rigor and motivation, student learning seems to thrive in a pass/fail environment when it is the *only* environment. Students are less concerned with grades and more concerned with achieving outcomes. But this does not seem to happen when a pass/fail option is embedded in a traditional grading system. That is, when some students are vying for high grades, most of those who need only pass the course aim no higher than that.

Pass/Fail Grading of Program Completion: A Promising Future

Competency-based education is a booming, large-scale form of pass/fail grading. Such programs may or may not have actual courses, but they all have tasks or outcomes, usually dozens of them, that students must perform at a high level of mastery to pass through them. These tasks are designed by professional test-makers. Students can practice the tasks as many times as they like, and they will receive feedback from faculty reviewers using precisely developed rubrics. If students do not achieve the highest level, they do not pass—call this a "gentle fail"—and must perform the tasks again and again until they do achieve it (LeBlanc, 2013). The standards to which students are held are high, but each attempt is low stakes. In the real world, however, no one has unlimited time to achieve a pass, which means that the stakes climb a little higher with each attempt.

Excelsior College, founded as Regents College in 1971, initiated competency-based education when it became the first institution to confer degrees based on evidence of prior learning. Established in 1972, New Jersey's Thomas Edison State College followed. Western Governors University (WGU), which delivers instruction entirely online to more than 25,000 students, has been conferring competency-based certifications and degrees since the late 1990s. At WGU, competency requires what administrators deem as B-quality or better work (Young, 2011). Other universities have since joined the ranks: Colorado State–Global Campus, the University of Maryland University College, Southern New Hampshire University, and about 20 others, plus the entire Kentucky Community and Technical College System. Now the University of Wisconsin System is promoting competency-based education to all its branches, including the Madison flagship campus. Even accreditation agencies are starting to get on board (Carlson, 2013; Field, 2013). However, the increasing popularity of competency-based education has motivated some pushback—notably from a bipartisan segment of the Missouri legislature that wants to protect the state colleges and universities, all of which assess student learning in traditional ways (Berrett, 2014b).

In vocational education, competency-based assessment focuses on pretty straightforward criteria: Does the student's weld hold under so many pounds of pressure? Does the vehicle pass inspection at all 25 checkpoints? Is the steak medium rare? But such competency standards may not be so obvious in all subjects. The faculty of Southern New Hampshire's College for America (CfA) devised ways to assess seemingly abstract competencies by breaking them down into smaller, discrete tasks. They developed an online associate of arts degree in general studies around 120 competencies representing the liberal arts and business studies, while abandoning the credit hour. Among these competencies are the abilities to speak persuasively or motivationally; devise multiple strategies to solve a problem; communicate information using graphs and charts; develop a budget; design a marketing plan; differentiate fact and opinion; and write a cohesive, grammatical paragraph (Kazin, 2012).

At CfA, students learn by doing. They are assigned a series of authentic tasks, each of which will allow them to demonstrate one or more of the 120 competencies, along with specific directions and online resources on how to perform each task. For instance, to show competency in writing a paragraph, students receive explicit instructions on how to do it: to introduce the main idea in the first sentence, to answer a specific question or two, and to offer examples to support their answers. For spelling and grammar, they are referred to online lessons. At a more advanced stage of the program, they must write a business memo recommending and justifying a certain course of action to their supervisor. The task requires and assesses analytic, integrative, evaluative, and writing skills as well as the ability to perform calculations using a spreadsheet program. Appropriate learning resources are provided. Alongside both of these tasks are the requirements for demonstrating competency, and these either mirror the directions or specify additional conventions that the work should follow (writing tone, word choice, clarity, etc.) (Kazin, 2012). The price tag for this self-paced AA degree is only $2,500.

Southern Connecticut State University offers a competency-based liberal education program built on eight competency pillars, including natural world, global awareness, creative drive, and cultural expressions. Students must display these competencies in certain assignments in their general-education courses. For example, to satisfy the cultural expression requirement, students must write an analysis that places an artistic work in context, explains how it creates meaning, and describes at least a few formal elements (Kennedy, 2012).

We can see then that competency-based education can be adapted to very different types of subject matter and programs. Perhaps in some areas it is long overdue. In professional fields such as medicine, nursing, and engineering, students should *have* to demonstrate high competency before passing a course or a curriculum. The cost of ignorance or avoidable human error is simply too high.

Perhaps not all the results are in yet on competency-based education because its widespread use is relatively new. It *seems* to be successful in the institutions that have adopted it, and it is beginning to become mainstream. But we really need a large-scale study that compares its impact on student learning to the impact of traditional programs.

Pass/Fail Grading of Assignments and Tests: Motivating Higher Student Performance

Whatever their employment situation, individual faculty have the discretion to grade assignments and tests pass/fail as long as they generate traditional letter grades at the end of the course. If we choose, we can raise academic standards and enhance our students' motivation to work. All we have to do is raise the passing bar from C or C– to the letter-grade equivalent of B, B+, or even A– work, as competency-based programs have. Then passing our course will demand a fairly high or very high level of skill competency and content mastery in the subject matter. It will actually require students to achieve the learning outcomes we set for them.

This idea may sound more innovative than it really is. It was introduced decades ago by Benjamin Bloom (1968, 1971) under the name of "learning for mastery" or "mastery learning." Developed for K–12 education, this model posits that all students can meet well-defined learning objectives as long as the teacher organizes them into smaller, sequenced units. The best teaching methods for accomplishing this goal vary from direct teacher instruction to collaborative learning to independent learning. Experimental research comparing mastery learning to traditional instruction has validated mastery learning as more effective. In fact, a major meta-analysis (Kulik, Kulik, & Bangert-Drowns, 1990) found that the mean effect size across 103 studies was just over half a standard deviation, which is a moderately large effect size.

This idea was recently resurrected for higher education by Kunkel (2002), who calls it "consultant learning." In his system, he grades individual assignments, not the course, pass/fail and gives credit only for excellent work—that is, A-level products—reflecting the standards of the real world. Any work of lesser quality receives no credit, and the student must redo it until it is excellent in order to earn credit. Students build a portfolio during the semester and receive a course grade based on the proportion of work that merits credit. According to Kunkel, this approach teaches students the importance of striving for excellence, which is what the real world rewards, if not requires.

More recently, Davidson (2009) has instituted pass/fail grading of assignments in her interdisciplinary studies courses, and she even lets her students do the grading (Jaschik, 2009). She determines the passing standards for each assignment, even creative ones, and allows students whose work fails the first time to revise it once. The number of assignments that pass on the first or second submission determines each student's course grade. Davidson favors this system because she finds it motivates her students to work harder and write more than traditional grading did.

Mike Pulley has enjoyed the same result shifting to pass/fail grading of just one assignment in his technical writing course. His students do a major team project based on a service-learning experience, and he requires them to submit a quality first draft that should have certain components. For years, almost all the teams turned in poor first drafts, even though Pulley graded them. Apparently, they expected him to tell them exactly how to salvage their draft and transform it into a fine product. Once he made the draft assignment pass/fail, however, most of the students did whatever they needed to earn a pass and the quality of the drafts shot up. So did the quality of the final product (Pulley, personal communication, December 3, 2012).

Psychology professor Dr. Cynthia Pury also grades just one assignment in her undergraduate methodology course pass/fail, and she does so because it is so time sensitive and critical. The assignment is to submit an acceptable proposal for an independent research project to the campus Institutional Review Board. Before she adopted the pass/fail standard, she encountered some students who did not take the requirement seriously and then could not proceed with or complete their research project. She had to fail them or give them an "Incomplete" in the course. Now all her students who do not drop the course early complete their research project and the course within the semester.

Even in today's traditionally graded classes, pass/fail grading is commonly used to give credit to certain assignments and tests, but not always under the pass/fail name. Students earn a certain number of points for turning in completed work or just displaying a good-faith effort and no points if they fall short. Instructors have added low-stakes homework assignments, in-class exercises, and short-essay quizzes to provide formative classroom assessments as well as incentives to attend class and do the readings (Nathan, 2005; Nilson, 2010). For example, physics professor Calvin Kalman (2007) has his students do daily free writes on the textbook readings to ensure their reading compliance and improve their comprehension. To help students become self-aware, self-monitoring learners, faculty have also introduced a wide variety of self-regulated learning activities and assignments requiring planning and goal setting, self-observation and reflection, self-testing and retrieval practice, or self-evaluation (Nilson, 2013). In addition, these assignments and activities allow students more grading opportunities without placing undue burden on faculty time.

Venditti (2010) uses a version of pass/fail grading when he assesses his students' public-speaking portfolio of the writing assignments and oral presentations they have done during the semester. His rubric has four criteria: completeness (all required items submitted), professionalism, writing quality, and the length and punctuality of the oral presentation. But unlike most rubrics, his does not describe multiple levels of achievement. Instead, he assesses each criterion of each portfolio as either satisfactory, earning 25 points, or unsatisfactory, earning zero points. An unsatisfactory on even one criterion lowers the portfolio grade considerably. Grading work pass/fail on multiple rubric criteria this way enhances student motivation (Rhem, 2011), which is not surprising. Because Venditti does not give partial credit, failure to measure up to a given standard costs dearly, so handing in incomplete or mediocre work is not a viable alternative.

What We Can Take From the Pass/Fail Research

For building a new grading system, pass/fail grading of assignments and tests provides an excellent foundation. Assuming we set pass standards at our current B level or higher, we immediately raise academic standards because students must submit at least B-level or better work to get credit. Grade inflation stops dead in its tracks. All the problems inherent in point systems—in particular, the time it takes faculty to decide on and justify partial credit and students' attempts to argue more points out of faculty—disappear. In addition, the evidence from faculty who have graded assessments pass/fail indicates that students perform at a higher level. They are more motivated and specifically more motivated to excel. Furthermore, because a performance is either acceptable or not, we can easily link it to one or more outcomes because an outcome is similarly a demonstrated-or-not proposition.

5

ESSENTIALS OF
SPECIFICATIONS GRADING

W ith the exception of pass/fail grading being an option in a traditionally graded course, the pass/fail system seems to be very
effective. So let's look at some details on exactly how it would
work for assignments and tests.

What are we really assessing when we are grading pass/fail? We are assessing whether a student's work meets certain *specifications*—that is, one or
more requirements that we set for a piece of student work. The work should
provide evidence of the student's achieving one or more course learning outcomes. If we shorten the term *specifications* to *specs*, we might think of the
way a piece of software is tested against certain specs. Some obvious ones are
whether the program runs, whether it does the task it was designed to do,
and whether it falls under a certain code length or operation time requirement. Either a program meets all these specs, or it doesn't. And if it doesn't,
it fails and must be revised or abandoned. Similarly, we can set specifications
for an assignment or a test. If the student's work meets (or exceeds) all the
specs, it earns a pass/full credit; if it doesn't meet all the specs, it merits a
fail/no credit. If full credit is five points, the work receives either five points
or zero points; partial credit is not available. To obtain any credit, a student
must read the directions and requirements carefully because failing even a
low-stakes assessment entails a cost, even if its total points comprise only a
small fraction of the course grade.

The notion of specs in the academy is not as alien as it may sound. Recall how competency-based education assesses students' achievement of learning outcomes. Essentially an institution sets the specs for a performance of a competency (or an outcome) at an acceptable high level of quality. A student either performs at that level or doesn't; the assessment is inherently pass/fail. More traditional colleges and universities also set general-education outcomes and their departments set program outcomes for their graduates. But these outcomes are generally less sharply defined and less rigorously assessed. They may be embedded in courses so that any students who pass these courses are presumed to have achieved all of them. However, merely passing a course does not guarantee competency in the promised outcomes—a reality already bemoaned in chapter 1. A student who slips through a composition course with a C probably does not write well at all. Even if he has improved, his sentence structure, grammar, punctuation, and spelling may leave a lot to be desired, and he may or may not apply what he has learned in the way he writes for other courses. This is why accreditors and employers do not put much stock in grades.

Specs and Rubrics

For assignments and tests graded pass/fail, students *have to* understand the specs. They must know *exactly* what they need to do to make their work acceptable. Therefore, we have to take special care to be clear in laying out our expectations, and we cannot change or add to them afterward. Because of the gradations in assessment levels, traditional grading approaches have not required instructors to explain their expectations so clearly before students begin the work. Until the introduction of rubrics, faculty might just have mentioned their grading criteria in passing and were not expected to furnish detailed guidelines for assessments.

Rubrics have represented a major step in getting us to articulate what we expect of our students. They make us write descriptions of descending levels of performance on each criterion on which we will grade a given work, which familiarizes students with academic language. Each level maps onto a number of points; a point range; a percentage; a percentage range; a letter grade; or a descriptor, such as *excellent, competent, developing,* or *unsatisfactory.* Being multilevel, rubrics seem to naturally complement the traditional system of giving letter grades at the end of a course. They also furnish formative assessments of in-process work, such as portfolios to be completed and products to be revised. They inform students about their level of performance in the skill areas targeted by the assignment or essay and help them decide how to divide their efforts.

You may find it useful to view specs grading as a system based on a one-level rubric with one criterion, but with that criterion being able to incorporate multiple requirements. Therefore, only one description is necessary as long as it incorporates all the required qualities. Only if a student's work has *all* of those qualities is it acceptable/satisfactory. As competency-based education shows us, outcomes assessment is inherently a pass/fail, satisfactory/unsatisfactory proposition based on a one-level rubric. Specs grading, then, aligns well with outcomes assessment, more tightly than rubrics do, and it holds students to high standards. As long as a course has multiple assessment instruments, and virtually all courses do, it can still generate a range of letter grades in the end. In effect, all the pass/fail grading systems for program completion and assignments and tests described in chapter 4 rely on specs grading.

As with rubrics, specs grading should not assess a work on every possible requirement we can conceive of. We should reserve this comprehensive standard for judging the scholarly work of our colleagues. For our students, we should carefully select a limited number of requirements that are really important for them to focus on and for us to assess in a particular assignment or test.

Setting Specs

Because specs grading raises academic standards considerably, students quickly learn the importance of following the directions and meeting the standards set in the one-level rubric. However, it also raises the standards for faculty in the area of communication. We take on the responsibility for providing students with all the information, instructions, and models that they need to succeed. Our specs have to be crystal clear, more so than the brief descriptions typically found in multilevel rubrics. This means taking the guesswork and mind reading out of the student experience, which will no doubt reduce student stress and enhance student motivation (see chapter 8).

What specs might we set? For typical, short homework assignments, the specs should be simple. For example, the work must do what the directions state and be complete, it must provide answers to all the questions, it must be at least a given number of words, it must show a good-faith effort, or all the problems must be at least set up and attempted. These specs define what is minimally acceptable to ensure that the students learn something important and take the assignment seriously. They supply sufficient direction for in-class assignments and typical daily homework, such as the kind designed to ensure reading compliance or self-regulation in the learning process.

In their book on journaling, Stevens and Cooper (2009) recommend this kind of grading for assessing regular reflective writing. They call it "power grading," and it involves only flipping through a student's journal to check that all the entries that should be there are there. In her course, Health Psychology, June J. Pilcher (personal communication, May 3, 2008) has obtained excellent results using very simple specs with more formal assignments. She has her students write 300- to 350-word summaries of the assigned readings focusing on one or two of the most important points and their connection to their life and experiences. Even her nonroutine assignments require few specs. She has students write biweekly reflection papers of 250–300 words on what they have been learning in the course and how they have been applying it in their everyday life. In her Management Information Systems (MIS) course, Kathleen Kegley (personal communication, January 5, 2009) assigns a wide variety of short writing exercises and has been very pleased with the work her students have submitted:

- In your own words, summarize the most important points of the _____ article in about ten sentences.
- Find and briefly summarize an article in the *Wall Street Journal* related to MIS.
- Search the web using "e-commerce" as a keyword, and find three sites that catch your attention. Describe each of these in three or four sentences.
- After reading the _____ article, pick out five new concepts that you learned and describe them in your own words.
- Read the _____ article and answer these two questions: What is distributed computing? How does it relate to screensavers?
- Choose two items that interest you on the _____ website and briefly describe the impact they might have on business.
- Read one other article at this website and summarize what you learned in five to eight sentences.

If you are not sure whether students understand your specs, show them a couple of examples of acceptable and unacceptable work. For instance, in Kegley's penultimate assignment, an unacceptable response would focus on only one website item, fail to identify a possible impact on business, or dismiss the website as containing nothing interesting. In the last assignment, writing fewer than five sentences on the article would merit no credit.

It is easy enough to write specs for fairly short assignments. But what about longer assignments such as papers, projects, and oral presentations? How can we compare those products with writing a piece of software, which has cut-and-dried, easily assessable *pass* criteria?

Where to begin? To start, determine what B-level work is. If you already have a solid rubric for an assignment, try collapsing the descriptions for the top two levels of work into one. Or you might consider just tweaking the top-level description. Another good idea is to recall the student errors that have resulted in point deductions in your traditional grading and transform these errors into specs that you can explicitly counsel your students to avoid.

A few examples illustrate how simple the process can be. Dr. Suzanne Waldenberger (2012) offers an array of short papers that her students can choose from to earn an A or a B in her Technology and Human Values course. For many of these, her specs include the length of the essay or presentation and a series of questions the work must answer. In his Scientific Skepticism course, Jeffrey Appling (personal communication, November 4, 2011) gives his students terse instructions for their case study papers: for those aiming for a C in the course, "600–1,200 words, modest depth—answer the question using what you learn in class and book; two additional resources cited (Internet okay)"; for those wanting a B, "1,000–1,500 words, C level plus more depth—additional resources (two non-Internet), related opinions, and personal reflection"; and for those aspiring to an A, ">1,250 words, B level plus *evidence* relating the impact of the topic on society." Among the assignments that Wayne Stewart (personal communication, November 7, 2011) requires of his students for an A or a B in his International Business course are reviews of five special issues of the *Economist* that focus on international business. Along with brief instructions on length, format, deadlines, and submission via Turnitin (turnitin.com), he provides basic substantive directions explaining the formula he has in mind: "1) summarize the essential points of the articles associated with the special issue, and 2) provide your reaction to those essential points, including a thorough and thoughtful assessment of the implications for doing business, particularly as related to concepts and discussions from the class."

Actually, most of the major assignments we make, especially at the undergraduate level—research or reflective papers, proposals, oral presentations, rhetorical essays, lab reports, and the like—ask students to perform a task that follows a formula or a template, and it is our job to describe this formula in plain language and sufficient detail for our students to complete the assignment to our satisfaction. It is also our job to show students at least a couple of examples of products that conform to the template and a couple of others that do not. In fact, models are essential for more elaborate assignments that students have not done before in your or other courses. With these models, students should be able to follow the directions we give for the organization, length, tone, references, and any other assessment criteria we have chosen and, in the end, earn full credit for the assignment.

Now let's consider a common, cross-disciplinary paper assignment: to write a review of the literature. Some courses make this task a learning outcome, often as background for a proposal, a rhetorical argument, an oral presentation, or a research study. When we assign a review of the literature, we implicitly mean a *good* one, one that meets at least basic scholarly journal standards. But to what extent do our assignment directions specify what the basic scholarly journal standards are? What exactly are those standards? Think about the better journals in your discipline, and within them, find some better literature reviews. About how many typewritten pages or words are these reviews? About how many references are cited? How recent are they? What are the reviews organized around—a controversy, a problem, a question, conflicting findings? What does the first paragraph say? What does the second one say? What logical conjunctions are used to highlight the relationships among the different works cited? How does the review end?

These criteria are not all low level, but they can be laid out and described. They are the stuff of routine professional scholarship, and we should be able to explicate them for our discipline. (Of course, after several years in the academy, we become so socialized into the template that we may have trouble articulating it.) We can also show students models of very good literature reviews and substandard ones, even if we have to make up the latter ones. If students study and discuss the models and follow the formula for references, organization, length, and all the other criteria, they should meet the basic professional standards and receive credit for doing the assignment. Conversely, students who fail to follow the formula will submit unacceptable work and receive no credit, at least not for that version of it if we permit a revision.

It is true that scholarship leaves a great deal to professional discretion and judgment, which a formula may not fully capture. Some scholars prioritize sound methodological decisions over other components of the research process, while others emphasize theoretical foundations, argumentation, or implications. If some research and writing decisions were not debatable, journal reviewers would never disagree. But these finer points reach far beyond our undergraduate students' professional understanding and need to know.

In the current grading system, we are not expected to lay out the template in such detail, so we don't. And our students do not always pay careful attention to the sketchy (to them) instructions they get. Besides, they can bank on partial credit for just making a weak attempt. No wonder the quality of the work they submit varies radically. We are willing to accept, "settle for," and give partial credit to work that falls short of what we define as good. In fact, we spend hours judging how much partial credit to give and writing explanations of each student's errors and omissions to justify our subtracting points. Most likely, we assess student work using a four- or five-level rubric. The top level describes a good review—for example, a first paragraph that explains the problem, subsequent paragraphs that summarize a collection of work making the same point, an organization that lays out the controversies or inconsistent findings in the literature, a certain number of references, certain kinds of references (e.g., scholarly journals and books and government reports), and a given number of words. Depending on your standards, the next level of quality may or may not represent what you consider to be a good review. If it does not, then the top level of the rubric furnishes your list of specifications for the assignment. If that second level of quality is still quite acceptable to you, then examine the third level. Chances are that this latter level is not what you would hope your students would submit. Grading as we have been using a multilevel rubric, you would give partial credit for work at this third level while knowing that it is not really satisfactory and does not reflect achievement of the learning outcome(s) it was meant to assess.

If this is the case, why accept unacceptable work? Why give any credit for it? It would be easier for us to give more specific directions when making the assignment. If we can write multilevel rubrics, which are more complex and arbitrary, writing a one-level rubric should save us time and effort. In addition, we might feel more honest awarding points only to student products that meet the requirements for good work and demonstrate the attainment of the related outcome(s).

Other scholarly and nonscholarly products follow formulas or templates as well, such as literary analyses, rhetorical essays, case debriefings, newspaper editorials and articles, research proposals and studies, business memos, business plans and proposals, financial statements, press releases, policy statements, engineering designs, and most types of oral presentations (sales, marketing, financial, persuasive and informative speeches, etc.). Each of these conforms to a certain organization and length limitation—or at least the good, clear ones do. Yes, some professionals purposely break the rules to make a greater impact, but students should not be violating the conventions before they master them.

What about creative assignments, exploratory work, and high-risk products? In fact, faculty should take advantage of the wider range of assignments and questions that a one-level rubric allows. While common forms of creative writing do follow a loose format, other creative assignments can still conform to certain standards without discouraging original thinking, risk taking, and exploration. Such criteria may include length (written or performed), purpose, audience, and anything else your learning outcomes may call for.

Few projects are more creative than the one Dr. Laura Gibbs (Rhem, 2011) assigns in her folklore courses. Each of her students develops a website featuring his or her own storybook, in which the student retells in the language of his or her own generation several ancient stories the students have studied. The rest of the class reads these updated stories. Of course, the students want to captivate their peers with great stories, but Gibbs does not grade them on that. In fact, she lets the students evaluate each other's stories by the feedback they provide. She grades instead with a relatively mechanical checklist that reflects the basic directions: having the required citations, responding to comments, including at least one image, proofreading the text, and the like. These are merely parameters within which students have complete creative freedom. They can get a good grade just by following the specs. Gibbs claims that grade anxiety, as well as the ugly behaviors that can come with it, never materializes.

You might choose to dispense with specifying the medium and organization and just offer alternatives. For example, consider the capstone assignment developed by Atlas (2007), which asks students to integrate what they have learned in the course in their own way and reflect on what they have gained. Certainly the task could be done in an essay, but it could also be done in a mind or concept map, a dramatic script or performance, pictures and images, or even an original song or dance. You could easily set specs such as these: it must address the task; it must include 10 major concepts (in this case you may or may not list specific concepts); if an essay or a script, it must be at least 1,200 words; if a mind or concept map, it must be at least four levels deep; and if a performance, it must be at least three minutes. Beyond these requirements, students can take risks, create art, or stay on the safe side with an essay.

"What if?" assignments and tests also call for creativity. Chun (2010) suggests a few that are embedded in authentic problems. "You are an adviser to State Senator _____ and have to research a controversial issue and formulate a policy statement"; "You are the class treasurer at your college and must prepare a persuasive recommendation for a given project"; "You are assistant to the director of operations at _____, a pharmaceutical company that has used animal testing, and must assess the accuracy of negative press and prepare a press release response." Kegley assigns this highly authentic writing exercise: "Suppose that you have just been hired by a prestigious company. Your new boss has asked you to submit a 12-line biography that highlights your professional strengths while still conveying some sense of your personality. What would you write?"

The possibilities are endless. The specs may be as simple Gibbs's mechanical checklist or Kegley's 12-line biography. Or they may be more complex, such as writing the requested document in 1,000 to 1,200 words, explaining your solution (policy stance, recommendation, press release) in the first paragraph, and making a three-point argument as to why your solution is the best possible. If you require outside research, specify the number and permissible types of references. If mechanics are important to you, give the number of allowable grammar, sentence structure, punctuation, and spelling errors. Then these are the only features you look for in your students' work and the only criteria on which you grade. Of course, you can provide other feedback and responses, but you need not concern yourself with points, partial credit, justifications, and corrections. Your students have plenty of room for their imaginations to play, and they may even read your comments more carefully because you have written them only to be helpful and constructive and not to justify your subtracting points.

If the notion of reducing assignments to checklists concerns you, take a look at Dr. Atul Gawande's 2009 book *The Checklist Manifesto: How to Get Things Right*. His examples come from the medical fields, air travel, and skyscraper engineering and construction, and there is nothing simplistic about the work done in these areas. As the book details, checklists alone have radically reduced the error rates of professionals. They can do it for your students, too.

Students, especially those in their first year, tend to significantly underestimate the time an assignment will require outside of class (Hazard, 2011). They can benefit a great deal from your time recommendations, especially for more substantial assignments. Time may also communicate to students how much depth of thought you would like them to demonstrate. Recommending that they allocate four hours to a paper indicates that you expect more evidence or more probing than two hours would suggest.

Adding Flexibility and Second Chances

Holding students to higher performance standards than those they are used to and eliminating partial credit will no doubt improve their work ethic but will also provoke considerable student anxiety, even if our expectations of their work are clear. As proposed in chapter 1, low student stress is one mark of a good grading system. Here we introduce safety-net mechanisms that instructors can integrate into their courses.

Most but not all faculty who use specs grading or something like it allow for limited revisions or "drops" of work that fails to meet the specs. On the one extreme, Kunkel (2002) requires that his students revise all their work until it earns an A. Mastery learning (Bloom, 1968, 1971) rests on similar practices. Some instructors do not allow revisions but do let students drop one or two unacceptable assignments from consideration in the course grade. In effect, Pilcher does this for learning logs and summaries of readings by requiring students to submit fewer than the total number of possible assignments. At the beginning of a course, students may not fully grasp the rigor that specs grading holds them to until they get back an assignment or two that receives no credit. For this reason alone, permitting and even encouraging early revisions or drops makes complete sense.

Perhaps the most flexible option is to set up a system of *tokens* (Kegley's term) or *free passes* (Pilcher's term). You allocate between one and five tokens to each of your students at the beginning of the course, and they are free to exchange one or more of them—it is your currency to control—for an opportunity to revise or drop an unsatisfactory piece of work, to take a makeup exam or retake an exam, or to get a 24-hour extension on an assignment. If you are using a point system (see chapter 6), students can use one or more tokens to have an absence from class *forgiven* (if attendance figures into your grading), to gain one or more extra points on a test or an assignment, or to obtain extra points at the end of the course. If you have eliminated points from your grading, you can take away tokens as a penalty for absences, late submissions, violations of classroom conduct rules, and the like. If you choose, you can furnish chances for students to earn tokens by submitting extra work or submitting an assignment at least a day early.

Depending on how you set up this economy, you may want to reward students for conserving their tokens until the end of the course. Those who consistently submit satisfactory work on time or early and do whatever else your system incentivizes may have accumulated a cache of tokens. They will have demonstrated the ability to defer gratification and avoid procrastination, and you may very well want to reward such self-regulatory behavior. If it benefits these students, you can double the value of tokens and let students exchange some high number of them for the right to skip the final or another comparable privilege. Or you may want to honor the student(s) with the most tokens with a gift certificate, book, trophy, or desirable artifact associated with the course material (Nilson, 2013).

An Assessment of Specs Grading Thus Far

Specs grading offers the following advantages:

- It dovetails smoothly into outcomes assessment because both are pass/fail propositions. Concomitantly, students shift their focus from points and grades to outcomes achievement.
- When faculty set the standard of acceptable work at a B or an A level, specs grading upholds higher academic standards.
- These higher standards paired with higher performance stakes motivate students to learn more and do higher quality work.

- Because students view the feedback they receive as decoupled from evaluation and no longer mere justifications for subtracting points, they are more likely to read it and take it to heart as constructive advice.
- Students experience less stress than they do now. One reason is that faculty make their expectations clearer. Another is that safety-net mechanisms such as tokens and the opportunity to revise or drop unacceptable work provide flexibility and second chances.
- The student-faculty relationship is less conflict ridden. Safety-net mechanisms eliminate at least some uncomfortable interactions, and, if the course expectations are clear and those mechanisms are in place, students are less likely to protest their grades.
- Specs grading enhances interrater consistency because raters have fewer ratings to quibble about.
- Specs grading requires less grading time than traditional practices, even with a rubric. Preparing a clear, one-level rubric should require no more time than preparing a four- or five-level rubric—and may even require less. During the actual grading, an instructor is only looking for certain features in a student's work, not fretting over how much partial credit to give and writing justifications for not giving full credit. Kalman (2007) can assess his students' daily free writes on the textbook chapters (see chapter 4), which are worth 20% of the course grade, because he is interested only in their being complete. As classes grow larger and teaching loads heavier, keep in mind that your grading time and your students' learning vary independently of each other.
- These time-saving advantages make possible more student-constructed assignments. This type of assignment can ensure reading compliance, foster self-regulated learning skills, assess students authentically, and both develop and evaluate their higher-order cognitive skills and creativity.
- Specs grading is simple and straightforward compared to our current system. The grading rubric for student-constructed work has only one level, and faculty need not make decisions about partial credit.

6

CONVERTING SPECS-GRADED STUDENT WORK INTO FINAL LETTER GRADES

As stated in chapter 1, specs grading does not challenge the institutional system of giving students final letter grades. This chapter shows two different approaches to organizing specs-graded assessments into course grades of As, Bs, Cs, Ds, and Fs in order to meet institutional requirements.

The Point System Alternative

In our traditional system, a student's course grade typically depends on the number of points that she accumulates across various quizzes, tests, and assignments during the course. Using a point system does not require instructors to give partial credit for incomplete or faulty work because they may grade an assignment as meriting all the allocated points or no points at all. In fact, this is exactly what Davidson (2009; Jaschik, 2009) does in her classes. She grades her assignments pass/fail, but each assignment is worth a certain number of points, and her students earn either all or none of the points. (She does offer an opportunity for revision.) Grades are determined by the number of points students accumulate this way.

For example, let's say the total number of points possible in a hypothetical course is 100, and grading is criterion referenced, such that 91–100 points merits an A, 81–90 a B, and so on. Of this total

- 17 points are for 17 specs-graded reading compliance and comprehension activities, each worth 1 point (homework, daily quizzes, in-class exercises, or recitation);
- 40 points are for four specs-graded written assignments worth 10 points each (e.g., case debriefings, policy analyses, research reports, treatment plans, literary analyses, lab write-ups);
- 8 points are for four specs-graded self-regulated learning assignments worth 2 points each (e.g., knowledge surveys, an essay on "How I Got an A in This Course," meta-assignments, postmidterm corrections/revisions, a letter to the next class, self-assessment);
- 10 points are for one specs-graded creative project (individual or small group);
- 10 points are for one traditionally graded midterm exam; and
- 15 points are for one traditionally graded final exam.

This grading setup is a perfectly reasonable *synthetic structure*—that is, mostly spec graded but with traditionally graded exams (see chapter 9). Instructors would wisely allow for revisions of at least two of the four specs-graded written assignments because one "unsatisfactory" would lower the final course grade by a full grade point. Or they might design 110 or even 120 points' worth of assignments and exams, some of which students could choose from to count toward the 100-point final-grade total.

This point-based grading strategy is indeed a viable, respectable option, but it might not be the best. Point totals do not easily map on outcomes. If a student earns 72 or 80 or 88 out of 100 points, that number does not indicate what she can and cannot do at the end of the course. In addition, students may not be in a position to choose the grade they will aim for in advance. Finally, the system is complicated enough to cause confusion.

The Bundling Alternative

The vast majority of faculty using specs grading eschew points for another more streamlined alternative. You have already come across it—groupings of assessments that are associated with final course grades—and you will see many more examples in the next chapter. So let's begin working with the terms *module* and *bundle* to identify the unit of work—a collection of assessments—that will be graded pass/fail. Each unit comprises multiple student products for which the instructor gives precise specs for satisfactory performance in a one-level rubric. *Modules* are units that are sequenced during the term, and *bundles* are units that students can complete in any order. The term *bundle* also serves as a verb meaning "to group" in the context of student assessments. Which student products to include in these units of work are among the basic course design decisions an instructor makes when implementing specs grading, and they can neatly tie into learning outcomes.

Bundling assessments is a truly innovative idea, one that holds some real advantages for both students and instructors.

Bundling to Simplify the Grading Structure

Chapter 8 discusses many ways to increase students' choices and control over the work they do to satisfy the course requirements. But when providing such choices, faculty may find themselves developing an array of assessment options that are difficult for both them and their students to keep track of. Bundles and modules furnish a structure for grouping these assessments in a logical way, and each grouping can link to a specific final grade. Rather than choosing among individual assessments, students can opt to complete a collection of assessments. With each option associated with a course grade, students in effect can select in advance the final grade they are going to work toward.

Bundling to Reflect Learning Outcomes

Bundles and modules can and should be designed for students to demonstrate attainment of specific course learning outcomes. Instructors can tailor each grouping to assess students' achievement of several such outcomes. The bundles or modules associated with higher grades might assess more outcomes, perhaps mastery of increasingly large bodies of material, or they might assess the achievement of more advanced, higher-level outcomes, such as the ability to perform higher-order cognitive tasks with the material, or both. For an example of such a grading scheme, the C-level module would assess students' ability to demonstrate knowledge and comprehension of the material, while the B-level module would require students to apply and analyze that material as well, and an A-level module would demand that students additionally demonstrate their skills in evaluating and creating with the material. In yet another scheme, the C-level unit of work might assess mastery of a specific body of content at all levels of thinking, and higher-level units would focus on mastery of larger bodies of content at all levels of thinking. Alternatively, each module or bundle might focus on one key learning outcome. If students must achieve one or more early-in-the-course outcomes in order to achieve later outcomes, then the units should be sequenced as modules. The following chapter showcases examples of bundles and modules with various links to outcomes.

To decide how to distribute learning outcomes among modules or bundles, an instructor must take into account other course-level design decisions, such as the relationships among learning outcomes, the availability of revision opportunities and tokens, and the procedures for determining final course grades.

Bundling to Add Learning Value

One reason to bundle is to increase the learning value of the core assignment. For instance, if an assignment is not particularly creative—let's say it's a standard research paper—faculty can enhance it with a creative dimension by having students mind-map or concept-map the entire paper or some part of it, such as the review of the literature. Or it may be possible to add a self-directed task to a standard assignment that can tap into the personal interests, intrinsic motivations, or career goals of the students. Or an instructor can offer a set of auxiliary or cocurricular activities to choose from, such as concerts, plays, performances, visits to a museum, or interviews of practitioners or leaders, that can add choice or even fun to a larger assignment, with no loss of academic value.

Other fruitful activities to attach to standard assignments and tests are *wrappers*, also called *meta-assignments*, that help students develop metacognition and become self-regulated learners. At the beginning of a course, an instructor might bundle one or more self-assessment assignments, such as a knowledge survey (Nuhfer & Knipp, 2003) or a self-assessment of the students' course skills or metacognitive skills (Cooper & Sandi-Urena, 2009; Schraw & Dennison, 1994), with their first problem set or case study analysis. Or to accompany a standard problem set, he might assign students some reflective writing on their confidence before and after solving each problem or have them do an error analysis of incorrect solutions after returning their homework (Zimmerman, Moylan, Hudesman, White, & Flugman, 2011). On papers and projects, students could enhance their learning, as well as the quality of the product, by also submitting a self-assessment or writing out their goals and strategies for the revision (Mānoa Writing Program, n.d.; Nicol & Macfarlane-Dick, 2006). Quizzes and tests offer some of the richest opportunities for exercises that develop students' sense of responsibility for their performance, such as postexam reflections, analyses, and game plans to prepare for the next quiz or test (Achacoso, 2004; Barkley, 2009; Zimmerman et al., 2011). Capstone assignments may invite accompanying reflections on what students learned in the course; how they learned it; where and why they encountered difficulties; how they overcame them; how their values, attitudes, or thinking patterns changed; and how they plan to use what they learned in the future (Costa & Kallick, 2000; Mānoa Writing Program, n.d.; Suskie, 2004). You can find dozens of options in Nilson (2013).

These side-dish assignments are not busywork. They add a whole new learning-to-learn and sometimes learning-to-care dimension to a course, which represents important student outcomes that the academy too often overlooks (Fink, 2003). They also increase the meaning and value of the content-oriented assessments with which they are bundled. Many of these assignments allow students to follow their own interests and increase their sense of volition and choice. Besides, students enjoy learning about themselves and their own cognitive and affective growth. This, too, is part of the higher education experience. Finally, as the last section points out, these wrappers can make the difference between academic success and failure for at-risk students.

As mentioned under the section "Pass/Fail Grading of Assignments and Tests: Motivating Higher Student Performance" in chapter 4, many faculty already use pass/fail grading for small assignments, such as written home-work and short-essay quizzes that give students an incentive for doing the readings (Nilson, 2010) and reflective, self-regulated learning activities and assignments (Nilson, 2013). But at this micro level alone, pass/fail grading does not drive major course design decisions, nor does it support any of the benefits of specs grading.

Bundling to Reduce Grading Time

Bundling can streamline the grading process and reduce grading time. To begin with, faculty need not calculate point totals. To obtain the grade asso-ciated with a bundle or module, a student must complete all the assessments within it at a satisfactory level. Instructors assess a set of related assignments as a whole. If any piece is missing or falls short of the requirements, they can stop reading. The set is not acceptable and may be returned to the student for revision and resubmission, if the course policy allows this. In addition, faculty can design bundles and modules to increase students' time on task and depth of learning without adding complexity to the grading structure. If an instructor made several related assignments separately, their number alone would complicate the structure for both the instructor and students.

To preserve our own sanity, we should schedule the due dates for bundles and modules, or for their component assessments, during the term. Imagine the nightmare of receiving a semester's worth of work during the last week of classes!

Consider this time-saving possibility that only bundling assessments can offer. If we offer students a total of, let's say, 10 modules, we can make suc-cessful completion of the first three the requirement for a D, the first five for a C, the first eight for a B, and all 10 for an A. Those students aiming for a D might submit all their work by the end of the fourth week of the semester.

Assuming their modules contain all satisfactory work and demonstrate their achievement of the most basic learning outcomes, they can pretty much ignore the class for the rest of the term. From then on, we in turn would have fewer students to grade. This is not as crazy as it may sound at first. Students with little motivation might start skipping classes at this point anyway, or if they do attend, they might drag down the pace and energy of the class. Wouldn't it be better to bid these students adieu and teach only the more motivated students as the material becomes more challenging?

Helping Students Succeed

Just as faculty should attach a recommended number of minutes or hours to each individual assessment they assign, they should do the same for entire bundles and modules and communicate this expectation to their students as early as possible. In fact, it is especially important to do this for bundles and modules because they are larger units of work, and students are more likely to underestimate the ultimate time commitment. This time information will help students make an informed decision about whether they want to take on the additional work required for a higher grade. Of course, the time each student will need will vary, and instructors should add a corresponding disclaimer to the estimated time for completion.

While we want and expect our students to successfully complete whatever bundles or modules they select, we have to decide how to handle unacceptable work and communicate the consequences of such work to the class at the beginning of the term. Even though such work may be rare, we should conduct a thorough "what if" analysis to anticipate the possible problems with submissions we may encounter and prepare ourselves to deal with them quickly, fairly, and consistently.

For instance, let's say that students have to complete the D-level and C-level bundles successfully before they can tackle the higher grade bundles. However rare this occurrence may be, what if a student who is aiming for an A or a B turns in an unsatisfactory piece of work within the C-level bundle? Should this "failure" prevent him from moving on to more learning and a higher grade in the course? We would hope not.

So here are some crucial questions we have to answer while designing a specs-graded course. Will we allow resubmissions? Or will we allow students to drop a poor piece of work from consideration? If so, how many revisions or drops will we allow during the term? Will they be limited to certain modules or bundles? Will we give students tokens that they can use for a resubmission or drop? If so, how many tokens, and how many can they use for resubmissions or drops throughout the term? How much time will we give students for a resubmission? However we resolve these issues, our answers belong in our course syllabus under grading policies.

Revisions can quickly get out of hand. Grading and giving feedback on multiple versions of assignments usually require inordinate faculty time, thereby eliminating one of the benefits of specs grading. In addition, the opportunity to revise can induce students to hand in substandard work initially. We should structure our courses to discourage student abuse of the options we permit. But at the same time, we need to accustom students to our new grading system. At first, they may not believe that sloppy work will receive no credit because they have not been held to such a rigorous standard in the past. So here is some advice. Option 1: We allow one revision of only the first assignment, and only then for students who turn it in early or on time. If we are bundling assignments and tests, we grant one resubmission of the first module or the lowest level bundle. Option 2: We restrict students' token usage for resubmission. If they start the course with, let's say, three tokens, they can exchange only one of them for the option to revise an unacceptable piece of work.

Providing feedback on unsatisfactory work can be as quick and easy as putting a check mark on the directions next to the specs that are missing or not adequately met, as Stevens and Levi (2012) recommend when grading with a rubric. Highlighting the specs will also work. This means, of course, that students should always attach the directions to their work. When we permit a revision, we may also have to tell students what they need to do to bring the work up to speed. But we should avoid dwelling on what is wrong with it; our check marks should be sufficient. Alternatively, we can give general feedback orally in class or in writing online because the shortcomings tend to repeat themselves across student work.

Grade Inflation

If students know what they have to do to get an A, won't all of them aim for and get an A in the course, creating even more grade inflation than we already have? As a result, won't administrators raise their eyebrows at higher average course GPAs and accuse faculty of pandering to student pressure for higher grades? These are perfectly reasonable questions, especially if you have noticed similarities between specs grading and contract grading, which decades ago gained a notorious reputation for giving students an A in a course for just about anything they submitted. Institutions reacted against it. Back in the 1970s, Towson University, for one, took measures to prevent grade inflation by requiring any faculty member using contract grading to obtain course approval from the Academic Standards Committee (Towson University, 2006).

To be fair, we must distinguish between two generations of contract grading. The original classic version arose at colleges and universities in the 1960s and 1970s. The contract was a two-way agreement between the supervising faculty member and each individual student about what that student would produce to earn the preferred grade, usually an A, in the course (e.g., Beare, 1986). Therefore, in any given course, the faculty member might develop 20, 30, or more different contracts. This system certainly did not save faculty time. In many cases, students set the standards for their own work independently, and faculty did not insist on the same standards across all students in a class. Under the name of "learning contracts," the system has endured until the present in the form of individually customized training and development programs for specific skills and a few community college degree programs (Boak, 1998; Sabin, n.d.).

More recently, a very different version of contract grading emerged. The contract is strictly one-way, developed solely by the instructor. To take the course, students must agree to it. It focuses on what work they must do to earn a specific letter grade in the course. In most cases, this involves a collection of work, much like a bundle but unrelated to learning outcomes. In other cases, grading is based on a point system in which each grade requires a certain minimum number of points at the end of the course. Students can choose from a menu of assessments, each of which has a point value. In general, students must inform the instructor early in the term what grade they will be aiming for in the course.

Whether the course relies on grade-based collections of work or a point system, each piece of work must meet certain requirements, which are in effect specs. While the instructor may grade some assessments traditionally, he will grade at least a few pass/fail, but only implicitly so because the syllabi for these courses make no mention of pass/fail grading. Because of the obvious parallels between specs grading and contract grading, specs grading started under the name of contract grading, and most of the course examples in this book were taught under this name.

However, the important differences between the systems justify distinguishing specs from contract grading. First, students do not tell their instructor that they are going for one grade or another. They wind up with the course grade that their work during the term justifies. Second, specs grading demands that faculty clearly and unambiguously explain their expectations (specs) of every assessment and requires that each piece of work be graded credit/no credit for meeting or failing to meet those specs. Third, specs grading raises academic standards by setting the passing bar no lower than B quality. Finally, it ties course grades to outcomes, at least when assessments are bundled, whereas contracts only rarely have (Andrews, 2004; Knowles,

1975, 1980, 1984, 1986). One more reason to differentiate specs grading is to avoid the apprehension about grade inflation that the term *contract grading* can still arouse in the academic world.

Fortunately, of the faculty who have practiced specs grading or the modern version of contract grading, only June Pilcher (personal communication, May 3, 2008, and January 20, 2010) reported giving more As than previously. But when she redesigned her traditional courses, she changed her assessments from largely exams to assignments and attendance. Jeffrey Appling (personal communication, November 4, 2011), Kathleen Kegley (personal communication, January 5, 2009), and management professor Steve Davis (personal communication, November 4, 2011) found no difference in their course grade distributions. In fact, there is no inherent reason why specs grading should reward any level of performance too generously. The standards for acceptable work are high, as recommended by Bloom (1968, 1971) in his work on mastery learning and Kunkel (2002) in his practice of consultant learning. Faculty are in total control of these standards for course grades. If they try specifications grading for the first time and obtain appreciably higher grades than with traditional grading, they should simply raise their standards the next time they teach the course. They can add more hurdles or higher hurdles.

Fostering the High Achievement of At-Risk Students

Not all students are likely to vie for an A. Not all of them need a high grade, especially in courses unrelated to their majors. Some may require only a C in your course to graduate and will aim just for that. Others may decide that the amount and challenge of the work required for an A are not worth the effort. As faculty, we should respect such decisions.

At the same time, we should encourage our students to strive for an A—in particular, underprepared and first-generation college students and students from underrepresented groups. These individuals are likely to underestimate their abilities and may lack the confidence to aim for high achievement. Furthermore, some of them may find college a strange and disorienting place, one that presents decision points they do not fully understand. If they opt for a lower grade and we do nothing, we are unwittingly reinforcing their misconceived fears that success is beyond their reach and that they really do not belong in college. Telling them personally that you believe in them and their capabilities may buoy their ambitions enough to make a huge difference in their academic success (Gabriel, 2008).

Still, encouragement is not the same as empowerment, and it may not make up for a substandard primary and secondary education. What *do* empower the students who most need a sense of self-efficacy are the self-regulated learning wrappers described earlier as a means to boost the learning value of assignments and tests. When these are assigned on a regular basis, they get students into the habit of monitoring their learning and evaluating the effectiveness of their reading strategies, their approaches to problem solving, and their study processes. These are practices that our strongest students may have started years ago, but our struggling students probably never have heard of them. In fact, research reveals that the latter students benefit the most from learning self-regulation (Ottenhoff, 2011).

The work of Zimmerman and his associates (2011) shows the powerful effects of two simple quiz and test wrappers on the performance of developmental mathematics students: first, self-assessing their confidence level before and after solving problems, and then completing a self-reflection form with an error analysis of the problems they missed. In the semester-long course, 68% of the students in the experimental-group sections with these self-regulated learning wrappers passed the course, versus 49% of the students in the control-group sections. The comparable percentages of students passing the gateway test allowing them to enroll in credit-bearing math courses were 64% and 39%. In an intensive summer course for students who had failed the gateway test on admission, 84% of those in the experimental-group sections passed the course, versus 63% of those in the control-group sections. In addition, 60% of the experimental-group students successfully completed a credit-bearing math course the following fall, versus only 34% of the control-group students.

Other associates of Zimmerman ran similarly structured experiments in an intensive summer developmental writing course for those who failed the gateway writing exam. In the postquiz revision sheets, students redid the writing task that the quiz assessed (summarizing, paraphrasing, etc.) and wrote reflections about where they went wrong during the quiz, how they prepared for it, and how they would better prepare for the next one. At the end of the course, 72% of the experimental-group students passed the gateway test, whereas only 52% of the control-group students passed. In addition, 65% of the former students successfully completed a credit-bearing writing course that fall, versus 32% of the latter students (Self-Regulated Learning Program, n.d.).

Another self-regulated learning assignment, designed for the first week of class, is the "How I Earned an A in This Course" essay. Zander and Zander (2000) created it as a transformative exercise to elevate the ambitions of underprepared, low-performing, or easily discouraged students, and several self-regulated learning proponents have incorporated it into their classes (e.g., Perkins, 2008; Wirth, 2008). Just writing about their high achievement as if it has already happened encourages students to set it as their goal and think about how they can reach it. Although the strongest students may simply take inventory of their most effective reading, writing, and studying techniques, lower achieving students will analyze why their performance has fallen short and then strategize how to improve it. This kind of introspective, analytical self-assessment, followed by devising ways to attain better outcomes, is integral to self-regulated learning.

Students may benefit from researching the matter. Among the many excellent resources available online, Wirth and Perkins (2008) highlight the behavioral differences among successful, average, and struggling students. Following this essay assignment with a class or small-group discussion can make other students resources as well. See Nilson (2013) for many more ways to teach your students self-regulated learning.

The wrappers featured in the Zimmerman experiments demonstrate that we can turn quizzes and tests into true learning experiences, and the first-week essay shows how we can help students aim for high achievement. Students will do this kind of postexam work and reflective writing on setting goals because they will quickly see its value and begin to benefit academically. This is genuine empowerment, and, along with our encouragement, this is what at-risk students need most to succeed.

7

EXAMPLES OF SPECS-
GRADED COURSE DESIGNS

This chapter displays and annotates a wide assortment of grading structures, with a focus on different ways that instructors can put together bundles and modules for final letter grades. The first section showcases nine courses from nursing, management, technical writing, communication studies, geography, psychology, and public health sciences. One of the nursing courses is at the graduate level. The second section shows three of the five bundles that Kathleen Kegley designed for her undergraduate course Management Information Systems. You may recall this course as an example of grading on more hurdles. Each bundle addresses a different MIS topic and assesses students' achievement on a broad range of outcomes, from lower-order knowledge and comprehension to creative problem-solving and self-assessment, on that topic. Students earn course grades according to the number of bundles they successfully complete by specific deadlines: a D for completing any three of the *Basic Learning Bundles* (Kegley's term), a C for completing any four, a B for completing all five, and an A for completing all five plus the corresponding *"A" Track* (Kegley's term) assignments. Only by completing all five bundles and the "A" Track activities can students achieve all six learning outcomes. It is worth looking at some of Kegley's activities and assignments because they are so varied, creative, and extensive. In fact, because this course is entirely online, her bundles constitute all the students' learning experiences.

Course Designs

The first course we examine is a graduate nursing course, Leadership in Healthcare Systems, developed and taught by Janet Craig, MSN, MBA, DHA, to prepare nurses for healthcare system administration (personal communication, November 7, 2011). At this level, the only passing grades are an A or a B, and she has a long list of outcomes on which she assesses all her students, whichever grade they pursue. A couple of them ask students to describe theories, frameworks, models, and the local healthcare system, but most are very high level: applying; analyzing; problem solving; developing strategies and recommendations; evaluating programs, departments, and organizations; synthesizing multiple resources; resolving ethical issues; and communicating effectively. Whether vying for an A or a B, all students must do the following:

1. Demonstrate preparation for and active participation in class discussions and activities.
2. Demonstrate presentation and writing skills consistent with graduate student work.
3. Conduct a scholarly multidisciplinary literature review of one self-selected organizational or leadership theory (guide provided). . . . Submit your plan and keywords for prior approval by the third week of the course.

Then for a B, students must also meet these requirements:

1. Write a group paper and make a class presentation demonstrating a comprehensive organizational, department, or program assessment with formulation of strategic objectives, alternatives, and recommendations customized to the community context; the organization's identified mission, vision, and values; and the health issues of the community's population. . . .
2. Demonstrate application of course content combined with critical thinking through preparations and presentation of one of the assigned healthcare cases in the textbook. . . . You may work with one of your class colleagues to benefit from peer review.
3. Pass all quizzes with a minimum average score of 75 and the final exam with a minimum score of 80. (You may eliminate one quiz score of your choice to raise your average score if necessary.)

For an A, students do an organizational, department, or program assessment with a different emphasis and somewhat more work in the form of a second case analysis and a summary of a book:

1. Write a group paper and make a class presentation demonstrating a comprehensive organizational, department, or program assessment applying course content and synthesizing external and internal assessments to arrive

at a SWOT analysis, critical success factors, recommended posture and positioning strategies, strategic goals, and recommendations for key value chain initiatives. . . .

2. Demonstrate application of course content combined with critical thinking through preparations and presentation of one of the assigned healthcare cases in the textbook, and do a written analysis of a *second* case. . . . (May be done with a class colleague.)

3. Select one of the books listed under "Selected Reading" on p. 7 of this syllabus and write an executive summary (2–4 pages) to share with the class. (May be done with a class colleague.)

4. Pass all quizzes with a minimum average score of 80 and the final exam with a minimum score of 85. (You may eliminate one quiz score of your choice to raise your average score if necessary.)

The additional work adds to the student's content mastery and provides more application practice.

We glimpsed at one aspect of this second course, June Pilcher's Health Psychology, in chapter 5 when we addressed how to set specs (personal communication, May 3, 2008). Here we examine her broader grading structure. For her students, their grades depend on the amount of work they complete, which reflects their content mastery. But their grades also take into consideration their class attendance and the timeliness of their submission of assignments. Their attendance is important because discussion is integral to every class meeting. Pilcher's syllabus sets out the following terms:

Assignments in this course will not be graded in the typical "point" fashion. Instead, each assignment will be graded pass/fail. The number of assignments that you pass will determine your course grade:

- Minimum requirements for an A:
  1. May miss up to two classes. Be on time and prepared for all other classes.
  2. Complete and hand in all bi-weekly reflection papers. (Students write 250–300 word reflections on what they are learning in the course and how they are applying it in everyday life). May hand in one paper late.
  3. Complete and hand in all summaries of assigned readings from *You* and *Health Psychology*. May hand in two sets of summaries late. (Students read the assigned chapter from *You* and write a 300–350 word summary of the two most important points of the chapter and relate the information to their life and experiences. Students also read one of the two articles assigned from *Health Psychology* and write a 300–350 word summary of the main point of the article and relate the information to their life and experiences.)

4. Complete the health behaviors project. Must attend April 30 presentations. (Students to apply the course material to their personal health-related choices by altering a health-related behavior in themselves.)

5. Read, summarize, and discuss *Optimal Human Being*. Must turn in summary and reflection no later than March 15. (Students write a 1,400–1,500 word summary and reflection relating the information in the book to their life and their expectations for the future.) Must attend class on March 29 to discuss the book with the other students who have decided to earn an A in the course.

- Minimum requirements for a B:
  1. May miss up to three classes. Be on time and prepared for all other classes.
  2. Complete and hand in all bi-weekly reflection papers. May hand in two papers late.
  3. Complete and hand in all summaries of assigned readings from *You* and *Health Psychology*. May hand in three sets of summaries late.
  4. Complete the health behaviors project. Must attend April 30 presentations.

- Minimum requirements for a C:
  1. May miss up to four classes. Be on time and prepared for all other classes.
  2. Complete and hand in all bi-weekly reflection papers. May hand in three papers late.
  3. Complete and hand in all summaries of assigned readings from *You* and *Health Psychology*. May hand in four sets of summaries late.

- Minimum requirements for a D:
  1. May miss up to six classes. Be on time and prepared for all other classes.
  2. Complete and hand in all bi-weekly reflection papers. May hand in four papers late.
  3. Complete and hand in all summaries of assigned readings from *You* and *Health Psychology*. May hand in six sets of summaries late.

Students must meet all requirements for each grade category to earn that grade. For example, if you miss one class, complete the health requirements project, read and discuss the *Optimal Human Being* book, complete all reflection papers on time, but turn in three sets of summaries from *You* and *Health Psychology* late, you will earn a B in the course. This may seem "picky" but I have to define clear criteria for each grade category and then hold to those criteria for this grading system to work.

The grading schema of the third course example, Dr. Janis L. Miller's undergraduate International Business Management course, also includes class attendance, but it is quite different from Craig's and Pilcher's. It combines a point system that applies to the exams and extra credit with additional assignments for grades of A and B (J. L. Miller, personal communication, January 11, 2009). To attain a B, students must meet the point and attendance requirements for a C and a D and write summaries of eight journal articles. Writing the summaries does not demand more advanced learning than performing decently on the exams, but it does extend the content mastery assessed. Only for the A, which requires a quality research paper, must students do more challenging work and achieve higher-level outcomes. Miller elaborates on her grading system and graphically illustrates it as a series of steps ascending from a final grade of F to an A, as shown in Figure 7.1.

> Students will earn grades based on the requirements that they choose to complete. In [Figure 7.1], students must complete all requirements at and below their chosen grade. For example, students who earn an A must complete requirements 1–7, students who earn a B must complete requirements 1–6, students who earn a C must complete requirements 1–4, and students who earn a D must complete only requirements 1–2. The incremental requirements for a higher grade must be completed at a correspondingly higher quality level, but the requirements for the lower grades can be completed at the corresponding level. For example, students who want to

Figure 7.1.   Graphic Depiction of the Grading System in the International Business Management Course Taught by Dr. Janis L. Miller

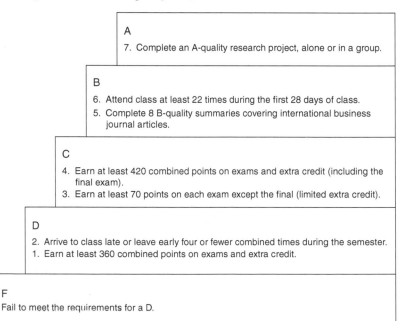

A

7. Complete an A-quality research project, alone or in a group.

B

6. Attend class at least 22 times during the first 28 days of class.
5. Complete 8 B-quality summaries covering international business journal articles.

C

4. Earn at least 420 combined points on exams and extra credit (including the final exam).
3. Earn at least 70 points on each exam except the final (limited extra credit).

D

2. Arrive to class late or leave early four or fewer combined times during the semester.
1. Earn at least 360 combined points on exams and extra credit.

F

Fail to meet the requirements for a D.

earn an A must complete an A-quality semester project, B-quality current event summaries, and C-quality exams, etc.

The fourth course example is Dr. Ardi Kinerd's Communication Design course (personal communication, August 15, 2011). Her ultimate outcomes for her students are introductory-level design skills for publication and a facility with the latest design software used in the publishing industry. Students receive higher grades for (a) completing more examples of a type of work, indicating that they have more practice in the required skills, and (b) completing higher quality examples requiring less revision, indicating that they have closely followed the presentation formula for this type of work. Here are passages from Kinerd's syllabus:

> Grades are assigned on a complete/incomplete basis, so there is no partial credit. All requirements for each grade tier must be complete in order to receive that grade. . . . All grade tiers require attendance and participation in in-class discussions and activities. Excessive absences will bring your grade down a letter. . . . If you do not meet the minimum requirement for a C in the course, you will receive an F.

- For a C in this course:
  1. Two individual projects
  2. One critique session (written and oral components completed to my satisfaction)
  3. A group project with one deliverable for a real client

Assignment quality: One or more projects need *major* revisions in order to look professional, be ready for print, or satisfy the client.

- For a B:
  1. Three individual projects
  2. Two critique sessions (written and oral components completed to my satisfaction)
  3. A group project with two deliverables for a real client

Assignment quality: One or more projects need *minor* revisions in order to look professional, be ready for print, or satisfy the client.

- For an A:
  1. Four individual projects
  2. Two critique sessions (written and oral components completed to my satisfaction)
  3. A group project with two deliverables for a real client
  4. A final group presentation of the client project deliverables

Assignment quality: All projects must be professional and ready for print. This means it should have little to no edits. Also, your client must be completely satisfied based on the written contract you and your client put together at the beginning of the project in order to receive full credit for the client project.

Our next course example, Dianna Conley's Travel Writing for Multimedia Platforms, aims to equip students to write for the travel industry, including creating and maintaining a travel blog and website (personal communication, September 3, 2011). As in Kinerd's course, students receive higher grades for completing more examples of a type of work, indicating that they have more practice in the required skills. But those who attain an A also achieve the additional outcomes of creating travel videos on a flip cam and posting these on a travel website. They will also have the experience of submitting two travel articles for publication and receiving a professional critique. Conley lays out her grading schema like this:

- For an A in the course:
  1. Complete four Travel Articles and submit one to www.TrekWorld.com. Two articles will be "how-to" articles with traveler advice and practical knowledge and the other two, creative/thought pieces that reflect on the student's own travel experiences. Students wishing to earn an A will chose one "how-to" article and one creative piece to be submitted to www.TrekWorld.com for critique by a travel professional and possible publishing on this website.
  2. Complete 15 blog entries.
  3. Complete a travel video in a small group.
  4. Prepare and present the Unique Destination Project. Many travel experiences will be done as a group, or pulled from a list of places prepared by the instructor. Once during the semester, each student will pick a place not on this list and prepare an article on visiting this location and a presentation "selling" this travel destination to the rest of the class.
- For a B:
  1. Complete four Travel Articles.
  2. Complete ten to 14 blog entries.
  3. Prepare and present the Unique Destination Project.
- For a C:
  1. Complete three Travel Articles.
  2. Complete seven to ten blog entries.
  3. Prepare and present the Unique Destination Project.
- For a D:
  1. Complete two Travel Articles.
  2. Complete three to six blog entries.

3. Prepare and present the Unique Destination Project.

- For an F:

    1. Fail to meet the D requirements.

The sixth grading schema we examine was developed by Dr. William Terry for his undergraduate Economic Geography course (personal communication, May 10, 2010). He says it plainly: "Essentially, the grade you receive in this course is completely up to you." The final grade depends on class attendance, which is central in this discussion-based course, and jumping more hurdles—that is, submitting more reflection papers on the readings and a longer topical research paper, both of which are evidence of greater content mastery. For an A, students also write an evaluative book review, which represents achieving a higher-level cognitive outcome than required of lower grades. To earn any passing grade, students must participate in class and select one of the following sets of minimum requirements:

- To earn an A:

    1. Maximum of two unexcused absences.
    2. Complete and hand in **all** (12) reflection papers (250–300 words), based on weekly reading.
    3. Complete a topical research paper and present it to the class (2,000–2,500 words).
    4. Receive a passing grade on two exams.
    5. Complete a 750-word book review (your choice, approved by professor) by April 1. In choosing this book, think about how you can evaluate the information presented in it like an economic geographer. There are many books today that cover topics as varied as globalization, labor migration, third world development, gender/class/race and employment, commodity chain, food production, and other relevant topics. Most of these books are not written by economic geographers, but . . . the themes you might find have some element of economic geography implicit if not explicit in the text. That is for you to evaluate. . . . It shouldn't be too difficult to find a book that is of interest to you. This is very important as I want you to be motivated to do the reading and write a thoughtful critique.

- To earn a B:

    1. Maximum of three unexcused absences.
    2. Complete and hand in **all but one** reflection paper (250–300 words), based on weekly reading.
    3. Complete a topical research paper and present it to the class (2,000–2,500 words).
    4. Receive a passing grade on two exams.

- To earn a C:
    1. Maximum of four unexcused absences.
    2. Complete and hand in **all but two** reflection papers (250–300 words), based on weekly reading.
    3. Complete a short topical research paper and present it to the class (1,000–1,500 words).
    4. Receive a passing grade on two exams.
- To earn a D:
    1. Maximum of four unexcused absences.
    2. Complete and hand in **all but four** reflection papers (250–300 words), based on weekly reading.
    3. Receive a passing grade on two exams.

Terry allows his students to use virtual tokens much the way that Kegley and Pilcher do, but he calls them "globes." Specifically, one globe can be traded for one missed reflection paper; one unexcused absence; an opportunity to revise an unsatisfactory reflection paper or topical research paper; or a 24-hour extension on a reflection paper, the topical research paper, or the book review.

The next three course examples come from undergraduate courses devoted exclusively to a research or community engagement project, some of which go on for several semesters. In the first two, note that one of the requirements for students to obtain any grade or even course credit is devoting so many hours per week to assigned project tasks. In the latter two courses, students have a great deal of choice about these tasks.

Pilcher teaches the first research-focused course (personal communication, January 20, 2010). The class meets weekly, and all passing grades require submission of weekly work summaries and a certain number of papers reflecting on the research experience, as her syllabus explains:

> Students on our team have the opportunity to be involved in research on the effects of stress and fatigue, research designed to improve patient care in hospital settings, and research on teaching effectiveness. The exact area in which students will assist depends on their interest and on what research is actively ongoing during each semester.

> Students will have the opportunity to be involved in several stages of the research process depending upon the number of semesters that they remain involved in the research project, including: literature search to find necessary background information, reading and critically evaluating background literature, data gathering, data management in Excel, data analyses in SPSS, and data presentation and publication. . . .

For three credit hours, students are expected to work approximately ten hours a week on assigned tasks related to our projects. For two credit hours, students are expected to work approximately seven hours a week. For one credit hour, students are expected to work approximately five hours a week. . . .

Students are required to turn in weekly summaries of the hours that they worked on our research effort with information on what they accomplished during each work period. I will provide a template to use for the weekly summaries. . . . Students will also be expected to complete a few reflection papers on their research experience each semester. . . . The course grades and their requirements . . . are based on three credit hours:

- Minimum requirements for an A:
    1. Work an average of nine to ten hours each week on assigned tasks.
    2. May miss one weekly meeting. Be on time and prepared for all other meetings.
    3. Complete and hand in all weekly summaries. May hand in two summaries late.
    4. Complete and hand in all assigned reflection papers. No late submissions will be accepted.
- Minimum requirements for a B:
    1. Work an average of seven to eight hours each week on assigned tasks.
    2. May miss up to two weekly meetings. Be on time and prepared for all other meetings.
    3. Complete and hand in all weekly summaries. May hand in three summaries late.
    4. Complete and hand in all assigned reflection papers. No late submissions will be accepted.
- Minimum requirements for a C:
    1. Work an average of five to six hours each week on assigned tasks.
    2. May miss up to three weekly meetings. Be on time and prepared for other meetings.
    3. Complete and hand in all weekly summaries. May hand in four summaries late.
    4. Complete and hand in all assigned reflection papers. No late submissions will be accepted.

The next undergraduate course, which combines research with engagement, is Health Promotion, Physical Activity, and Obesity Prevention in Children, Adolescents, and Teenagers, taught by nursing professor Dr. Janice Lanham (personal communication, August 26, 2011). Her syllabus states that by the end of the research project students should be able to "develop, implement, and evaluate a culturally appropriate and linguistically competent community health promotion and disease prevention program [emphasizing] physical activity/fitness, nutrition, and weight management for children, adolescents, and teenagers" in large minority population communities. To achieve this ultimate outcome, students will learn how to do the following along the way:

1. Increase community consciousness about health promotion, physical activity, and obesity prevention.
2. Collaborate with community partners to develop and implement targeted outreach to children, adolescents, and teenagers at risk for obesity.
3. Follow best practices to promote physical activity and healthier lifestyles in the target populations.

Lanham's grading structure looks very different from those of the other courses we have examined, and it offers students a tremendous range of choices. All students hoping to pass with at least a C must do the following:

- Attend course meetings, missing no more than two.
- Earn a passing score on CITI (Human Subjects Research) training.
- Conduct a comprehensive literature review (minimum 25 references).
- Make a poster presentation.
- Submit an ePortfolio with student reports and other evidence of completed activities.

To earn a B, students must complete *any two* of the following tasks. To earn an A, they must complete *any four* of these tasks. In other words, they can choose the parts of the project that interest them.

- Develop a case scenario.
- Meet with research participants.
- Compile data.
- Produce a podcast presentation.
- Participate in running focus groups.
- Develop an online survey.
- Collect data.
- Collect visual or audio media.
- Evaluate the media you collected and summarize your findings in writing.
- Prepare an annotated bibliography of the literature review (minimum 25 references).

The last course, called Healthy Communities Initiative, combines field-work with engagement. It is cotaught by Will Mayo, Susan Pope, and Jennifer Goree, all of whom are nonfaculty specialized in various facets of health and wellness (W. Mayo, personal communication, August 26, 2011). According to their syllabus, their students will learn how to promote the adoption of healthy lifestyles among individuals and populations on a college campus. The grading system resembles that of Lanham's in that to pass the course all students have to do a list of activities and their choice of two or four activities from another list to earn the grade they want. These are the required activities for all students:

- Complete and submit a personal wellness profile during the first weekly meeting of the class.
- Complete and submit a personal fitness assessment by a given date.
- Complete and submit personal challenge activity logs on a weekly basis.
- Complete and submit a personal challenge reflection journal on a weekly basis.
- Attend weekly class meetings, missing no more than one.

Students aiming for a C must satisfactorily complete two activities from the following list of options, those pursuing a B must complete two, and those vying for an A must complete four:

- Attend Alcohol Skills Training Presentation (ASTP) offered during the semester.
- Contact and interview one campus program representative related to health and wellness.
- Research any key area of campus health and wellness (list provided) and write a summary of the major findings; must use at least three peer-reviewed articles.
- Assist the campus recreation center with its annual survey by completing one hour as an interviewer.
- Administer the Health Interest Survey for one hour at the campus employee benefits fair.
- Contact and interview one faculty member who conducts health-related research to find out how he or she defines health and wellness and what he or she studies.
- Attend three campus programs related to health and wellness (examples provided).
- Complete any other activity related to health and wellness not on this list that is pre-approved by one of the instructors at least a week in advance.

Extensive Bundles

Here we look at three of the five bundles of assignments that Kegley designed for her undergraduate course Management Information Systems. Each bundle asks students to complete activities that range from the lowest-order to the highest-order cognitive outcomes, but each on a different MIS topic. Recall that course grades depend on the number of Basic Learning Bundles students successfully complete by specific deadlines: a D for completing any three, a C for completing any four, a B for completing all five, and an A for completing all five plus the corresponding "A" Track assignments. How many of the six possible learning outcomes students achieve also depends on the bundles and "A" Track activities they complete (see chapter 3 for the list of outcomes). Because these bundles constitute the entire online course, they illustrate the wide variety of learning experiences that instructors can provide. All of them are hands-on. Note that Kegley provides the recommended length of time for each activity. Before exploring the bundles, let's read a few passages from her introduction to the course:

> Management Information Systems (MIS) involves the effective design, delivery, and use of information systems in organizations. It encompasses many different areas such as computer science, management, accounting, marketing, and economics. My teaching philosophy, which is anchored in adult learning theory, is that you can best learn these concepts by doing hands on activities. Much like three blind men experience different parts of an elephant, the Learning Modules are designed to show you different aspects of MIS (www.noogenesis.com/pineapple/blind_men_elephant .html). I promise you that the activities are designed to meet learning outcomes and are not "busy work." If you ever find yourself doing an activity in this class and you're not sure what it is supposed to accomplish, don't hesitate to let me know. I read each word of your work and appreciate a good effort and independent thinking.

> The course will consist of five Learning Bundles, each of which has a hard-and-fast due date. These dates are spread throughout the term because you will learn better by making a continuous effort over many weeks than by cramming all your learning into one long weekend. Each Learning Bundle has two components: a Basic Track that is estimated to require ten hours of effort and an optional "A" Track project that requires at least three additional hours of effort per bundle. For an "A," you need to devote a minimum of three hours per bundle to demonstrating your learning about a software package. Please don't hesitate to talk to me (e-mail, phone, in

person) to make sure you understand what I'm asking for in the projects, which is a good solid effort and documentation of your learning. . . .

Rather than taking traditional exams, you will create a mind map at the end of each bundle to allow you to demonstrate your knowledge, as well as a chance to reflect, synthesize, and review the material to help it become more useful to you.

Learning Bundle 1: Foundation Concepts

This bundle reviews some basic concepts related to MIS as well as other foundations essential to the class. To relate these concepts to the real world, one component will focus on reviewing current articles that relate to MIS. . . . Another thread in the topics will be innovation because of the tremendous potential and impact of innovative uses of information technology. For this purpose, you will study the first four chapters of *Thinkertoys*. As in any professional, adult-learning-theory–based class, self-assessment is an important component. The module concludes with an activity that asks you to create a mind map of Management Information Systems as your own assessment of your learning.

Please note that each component is estimated to take two hours. . . . The estimation is to help you be aware of the level of effort expected. At the end of the assignment, you will be asked to estimate the time you spent on the module, so please make an effort to keep track. Turning in sloppy work that took five minutes to complete will be obvious. While one component may take more or less than the two-hour estimate, the overall effort should take about ten hours. If you find that you are spending much more time than this, contact me so we can talk about it.

This learning experience is designed to be fun, safe (with respect to grading), informative, and rewarding. You should feel that you have accomplished significant learning after you complete the module. . . .

Basic Module (items 1–5): For all students. Credit will be awarded if your product illustrates *all* of these qualities:

- Sound academic effort, as measured by completeness and attention to detail
- Professional presentation, meaning that text and visuals have a neat and well-organized appearance
- Synthesis of ideas in your own words

1. Review Concepts (2 hours). The learning objectives for this portion of the module are to provide a review of some basic concepts you have probably encountered in other classes, as well as to provide a valuable resource for many topics in the "howstuffworks" website. I purposely chose the word "browse" to indicate I don't expect you to memorize these articles. They probably contain more than you want or need to know. Instead, look over them to increase your knowledge of basic computer concepts. This will help support learning about related concepts as we progress through the class (even if you can't remember the terms, you will have a good resource for reference if you need it).

   1.1. Software: Browse the article at http://computer.howstuff works.com/bytes.htm. What is the ASCII character set? Write your first name using the ASCII character set, leaving a space between characters.

   1.2. Microprocessors: Browse the article at http://computer .howstuffworks.com/microprocessor1.htm. Describe in your own words five new concepts that you learned from this article.

   1.3. Neat Stuff: Browse the article at http://computer.howstuff works.com/screensaver.htm. What is distributed computing, and how can it relate to screensavers?

   1.4. The Future: Browse the items at http://computer.howstuff works.com/ces2004.htm. Choose two items that you find interesting and briefly describe the impact they might have on business.

   1.5. Your Choice: Select and browse one other article at http:// computer.howstuffworks.com. Then describe what you learned in five to eight sentences.

2. Learning Styles (2 hours)

   2.1. Complete the questionnaire at www.engr.ncsu.edu/learning styles/ilsweb.html. For one of your traditional classes, guess your instructor's learning style based on his or her teaching style, or if you prefer, ask the person to complete the questionnaire. Read the information at the website www.ncsu .edu/felderpublic/ILSdir/styles.htm, and indicate how your learning style compares to the instructor's and how you can compensate for any differences. Please turn in your questionnaire results, your guess of your instructor's style (using the same format as your results), and a brief discussion of how you can compensate for the differences.

   2.2. This course is based on adult learning theory. Please read the following article: http://agelesslearner.com/intros/andragogy

.html. Using this article and others you wish to read—do a keyword search using "andragogy"—describe the basic concepts of adult learning theory and indicate at least three ways that the structure of this course adheres to the principles of the theory.

2.3. Visit the website www.mind-map.com/EN/mindmaps/definition.html to learn about mind maps and the rules for creating them. Visit the mind map gallery to see some examples, noting the use of symbols, color, and expressive text to represent and connect concepts. The underlying theory is based on your brain's associative nature and the impact of visual information. Mind maps can be used for presentations, learning new material, reviewing for exams, and other purposes. To better acquaint yourself with mind maps, interpret the mind map MindMap.ppt in this electronic folder by stating in ten to twelve sentences what this mind map is trying to convey.

2.4. Suppose that you have just been hired by a prestigious company. Your new boss has asked you to submit a twelve-line biography that highlights your professional strengths while still conveying some sense of your personality. What would you write?

3. What's in the News? (2 hours). This section will help you relate the basic concepts to real world topics. It also points you to different "portals" for gaining current information about the use of computers in business.

3.1. For this short article, summarize the key points in your own words (about ten sentences): "Ten Stories That Rocked (OK, Touched) Your World" at www.computerworld.com/article/2574145/it-outsourcing/ten-stories-that-rocked--ok--touched--your-world.html

3.2. Browse an issue of the *Wall Street Journal*; extra copies are often available in the Academic Advising office. Select an article that is in some way related to MIS/computers in business and briefly summarize it.

3.3. Go to the *ComputerWorld* website at www.computerworld.com. Browse the list of topics, and select an article in an area of interest to you. Read and summarize the article in about ten sentences.

3.4. Visit the website www.monster.com and do a job search using the key term "MIS." Read over a few of the job descriptions related to MIS. What are some general responsibilities and requirements that are related to MIS careers?

4. Thinkertoys (2 hours). Information systems are a tremendous potential source for innovative ideas. . . . Read Chapters 1–4 in *Thinkertoys*.

Remember, you are not going to be tested on this material. Instead, you should address the material as a foundation for future exercises that will enhance your creativity. . . .

4.1. Do the Tick-Tock exercise on page 5. You do not need to turn this in, but please indicate that you have done it. How does this exercise relate to the FLY WIN image on page 7?

4.2. Look at the image on page 10 for THE CAT. Notice how your mind fills in the identical letters in a different way based on expectations. With this in mind, do the Creative Affirmation exercise on page 9, middle of the page. Specifically, write down several affirmations about your own creativity. Then, as the text explains, write down 20 variations of one affirmation. Again, I consider this personal and am not asking you to turn it in; just please do it and indicate that you have done it.

4.3. Suppose your challenge is to create a new marketing advertisement for umbrellas. How can you create an ad that really stands out from the others? Chapter 2, "Mind Pumping," gives ten ways to pump your mind for ideas. Choose three of these that appeal to you the most and give them a try. Write a brief description of what you did and what results you obtained.

4.4. Before looking for ideas, have a goal in mind. Chapter 3 identifies general business problems and converts them to specific challenges. Why does the author insist it is useful to write the challenge down? Write the challenge from question 4.3 above and rewrite it several times using the Blueprint on page 28. This isn't personal, so turn it in. The idea is for you to get experience manipulating a challenge so that you can look at the problem in different ways.

4.5. Chapter 5 is about Thinkertoys. What are Thinkertoys?

5. Self-Assessment (2 hours). An important component of adult learning is the involvement of the learner in assessing their progress. A mind map is an excellent way to do this, since it requires you to "synthesize" or bring together ideas, concepts, and relationships that you encounter from different sources.

5.1. Create a mind map that illustrates the concept "Computers in Business." Please note that there is no "right" answer; the idea is to help you formulate and internalize the material that you have been learning about. One approach is to take a big picture view of the different concepts you have encountered and find a way to structure and interconnect them. For example, one branch of your mind map might be "Computer Basics" where you diagram the information learned in step 1 of the module. Also include the Thinkertoys concepts/exercises in your mind map. Be sure and use expressive text, colors, illustrations and symbols in your mind map because these engage many different portions of your brain in the learning process and help make the information more usable for you in the future. Note that your mind map will be highly individual. Do not feel like you are supposed to have a "right" answer.

5.2. Please indicate how much time you spent overall on this module, and note any extreme exceptions (any assignments that took far too long or much less time).

"A" Track Option (item 6): Only for students on the "A" Track. Serious commitment to the project is clearly obvious. Submission of work that fails to meet this criterion will result in automatic withdrawal from the "A" Track option. Specifically, you cannot turn in an unacceptable effort with the project and remain on the "A" Track, which is consistent with real-world projects. If you are serious about the project and the grade, I will work with you to help make sure you get the results you want and are willing to work for.

6. Learning to Learn Technology (3 hours). Identify a technology related to MIS that interests you, such as Macromedia, Dreamweaver, or Flash. The goal is for you to gain a total of fifteen hours [of] hands-on experience in an area that will support your career goals. The project emphasizes "learning how to learn"; it is not a term paper. Please have your software choice approved before investing time in learning about it because some packages are too simple to support the goals of the project. Determine how you will obtain this technology (download a trial version? purchase?). Find resources that will support your efforts to learn the technology, such as online tutorials, books, and workshops. Make sufficient progress to fulfill your obligation of three hours.

6.1. Write a one-page proposal that includes the information above as well as any progress that you have made on your project (include any prototypes, tutorial results, etc.). Show that you have found a learning path customized to your chosen software package. Think of it as trying to prepare you for the day your new boss says, "We need someone to take the lead in (insert leading-edge software package completely unfamiliar to you). Hey, why don't you take a few weeks to learn this software then come back and report to us what you've learned?"

6.2. Document the amount of time you invested in the project.

Learning Bundle 2: Information Technologies

This bundle, Information Technologies, contains two very important topics, Data Resource Management and Telecommunications/Networks. It consists of five components in the basic module, which is for all students, and one additional component for students in the "A" Track. The first two components should give you a foundation of the basic concepts, and the third introduces you to current topics in the news. As in the previous bundle, the fourth component uses the *Thinkertoys* book to help you develop your creativity and apply to business challenges. Finally, the fifth component asks you to create a mind map that synthesizes what you have learned in this bundle. The basic track should take a total of about ten hours. If you are participating in the "A" Track, you will need to do an additional three hours of work to demonstrate your progress in your project. Please let me know if a task is taking longer than it should or if you find a broken link. *Basic Module (items 1–5): For all students.* Credit will be awarded if your product illustrates *all* of these qualities:

- Sound academic effort, as measured by completeness and attention to detail
- Professional presentation, meaning that text and visuals have a neat and well-organized appearance
- Synthesis of ideas in your own words

1. Basic Concepts—Data Resource Management (2 hours)

   1.1. Visit the tutorial at www.geekgirls.com/databasics_01.htm and get an idea of what a database is. In your own words, summarize the differences between a database and a spreadsheet. Then visit the site www.ferryhalim.com/orisinal. Explain how a database might be used to support this site. What are some likely tables and their content? What are some likely fields in the tables you propose? There is no single right answer; just show that you've read the article and have thought carefully about these questions.

   1.2. View the presentation and notes in Case_Studies.ppt, and read the case study about Experian. How do the database software tools discussed in this case help companies exploit their data resources? Describe three other business opportunities that you could recommend to Experian that would capitalize on their automotive database. Be sure to look at the Automotive section of the corporation's website (www.experian.com/business_services/index.html) to help you answer.

1.3. Read the case study on slide 28 of the presentation Case_Studies .ppt. List three challenges in acquiring and using data from external sources identified in the "Sherwin-Williams and Krispy Kreme: Managing External Data Sources" case. Explain how the approach to acquiring external data differs for Sherwin-Williams and Krispy Kreme, and state an advantage and disadvantage of each approach.

1.4. Visit the website www.alphasoftware.com. Suppose you have selected this software for your company. Write a short (about ten-sentences) memo to your boss recommending that the software be purchased, including the features and criteria that you think are the most important for your particular company. You can choose the company type and size.

2. Basic Concepts—Telecommunications/Networks (2 hours). The resource for this topic is the Cisco tutorial website, which is oriented toward practical knowledge. Suppose that you have just decided to start your own small business, but only have a general idea about telecommunications and networks. To learn the basic building blocks you will need to be familiar with as you develop your company, go to the [following website] and answer these questions: www.cisco.com/warp/public/779/ smbiz/netguide/i_bldg_blocks.html. Note the navigation box to the right; first visit the Building Blocks section, then visit the Network Technologies section to complete these questions. . . . State the answers in your own words. . . .

2.1. What are the five components that most computer networks have?

2.2. How are hubs and switches similar? How do they differ? Which would you use for your company, and why?

2.3. What is the Client/Server Model? How does it differ from the Peer/Peer Model. Which would you use for your company, and why?

2.4. What are the three main types of wiring? What are some selection criteria you would consider before choosing a particular type of wiring for your business?

2.5. What is a collision? What is the difference between Shared and Switched Ethernet technology?

2.6. What role have standards played in wireless technology?

2.7. What are LAN and WAN? Why is network design aimed at keeping as much communication traffic as local as possible?

2.8. Why is digital communications preferred over analog communications?

2.9. Which network technology (for example, ISDN, analog lines) would you choose for your business's remote access (wide area) network? Explain your choice.

2.10. What are some advantages of Virtual Private Networks as compared to WANs? Would you consider the former for your company? Why or why not?

3. What's in the News? (2 hours). The article "Oracle Eyes Windows Database Market" gives a snapshot of current events in MIS and introduces some terms worth adding to your MIS vocabulary. Read it at: www .computer world.com/databasetopics/data/software/story/0,10801,895 27,00.html?SKC=data-89527

3.1. List three key points from the article.

3.2. One term in the article is "grid computing," which . . . should sound familiar from LM1. Visit www-1.ibm.com/grid/about_ grid/index.shtml# to get an idea of how IBM is promoting the use of grid computing in business. Go to *Gridlines* to see different applications of grid computing (www-1.ibm.com/grid/ gridlines/January2004/?ca=gridlines&me=W&met=inba&re= gridhp). Choose one of the applications in Industry Trends, and briefly describe how grid computing is being used. How do you suppose grid computing is related to databases?

3.3. This exercise is to introduce you to the concept of Linux and open source software. First visit http://en.wikipedia.org/wiki/ Source_code to get an idea of what is meant by "source" code. Then read the article at http://liw.iki.fi/liw/texts/linux-the-big-picture.html. What motivated the development of Linux, and what is meant by "open source" software?

3.4. Visit the website www.computerworld.com/networkingtopics/ networking?from=left, which contains telecommunications news. Read any three articles of your choice. For each article, give the article name and write in three to five sentences a brief summary of it or identify points of interest to you.

4. Innovate or Die! (2 hours). Many companies acknowledge that innovation is crucial to business success, but few people are actually familiar with the creative process that is required for innovation. In this section, you will continue with the *Thinkertoys* text and actually apply some of the creativity techniques to a specific challenge. The challenge will be based on a service-learning experience, and your ideas will be collected and given to the new group on campus . . . to help the organization increase attendance at meetings or events, donations, or volunteers.

4.1. Become familiar with Chapter 5 in *Thinkertoys*, which includes several examples illustrating how this technique has actually been used in business. Select the example that you think best illustrates the technique or has generated the most innovative solution and briefly explain your choice. Then follow the blueprint on page 45, and turn in your responses for each of the steps for the given challenge. Please give at least five specific innovative recommendations for the challenge based on your use of this technique.

4.2. Become familiar with Chapter 6 in *Thinkertoys*. Several examples are given illustrating how this technique has actually been used in business. Select the example that you think best illustrates the technique and/or has generated the most innovative solution and briefly explain your choice. Use the blueprint on page 55, and turn in your responses for each of the steps for the given challenge. Give at least five specific innovative recommendations for the challenge based on your use of this technique.

5. Self-Assessment (2 hours). Create a mind map on your computer that reflects and brings together what you have learned in this bundle. Your central "starting point" should be Information Technologies, and you should have a branch for both Data Resource Management and Telecommunications/Networking. . . . As before, use colors, icons, symbols, and pictures to distinguish the concepts in your map. Include at least 30 concepts and at least 30 graphics that reinforce these concepts.

"A" Track Option (item 6): Only for students on the "A" Track

6. Show Your Learning (3 hours). Demonstrate that you have invested at least three hours of your time in your software project. You may include screenshots or prototypes of your work or demonstrate your efforts in some other way. . . .

Learning Bundle 3: Electronic Business Applications

This bundle focuses on electronic business applications and these important concepts: e-business and e-commerce (not the same); functional business systems (that is, software to support marketing); integrated enterprise business systems that connect all the different functional areas of a business (that is, Enterprise Resource Planning, or ERP, software); decision support software (DSS) to assist managers with forecasting, predicting, and making strategic business decisions; and artificial intelligence (AI), which has business uses. You will visit ELIZA, one of the earliest classical artificial intelligence systems that acts like a therapist.

Basic Module (items 1–5): For all students. Credit will be awarded if your product illustrates *all* of these qualities:

- Sound academic effort, as measured by completeness and attention to detail
- Professional presentation, meaning that text and visuals have a neat and well-organized appearance
- Synthesis of ideas in your own words

1. Basic Concepts—E-Business (2 hours)

   1.1. Functional business systems focus on a particular aspect of the business. For each of five types of functional business systems, find one example on the web of software that claims to support the business function. List the software name and a short description (2–3 sentences) of what they claim to provide. The systems are marketing, human resources, financial management, manufacturing, and accounting.

   Cross-Functional Enterprise Systems are "integrated" systems that connect the different functional aspects of business. With isolated functional systems, companies are finding the "failure to communicate" across functional areas devastating. Read the Case Study 3, Union Pacific, Corporate Express, and Best Buy: Enterprise Application Integration Challenges, which is provided as a Word document in this folder named Case Study 3, and answer the following related questions (1.2–1.4).

   1.2. What are the major advantages and challenges faced by businesses that implement EAI initiatives?

   1.3. Webmethods is a company mentioned in the case study. Visit the Webmethods website at www.webmethods.com and choose one of their customers' success stories (click on Customers to get a drop down menu with Success Stories as one option) to read. List what you believe to be three key points from the case study.

   1.4. One of the challenges faced by Best Buy is "data mapping." What do you think this means within this context? There is no right or wrong answer; the goal is for you to think about it and summarize in four or five sentences what you think it could mean.

    1.5. Search the web using "e-commerce" as a keyword, and briefly describe three sites that you find interesting (three or four sentences each).

2. Basic Concepts—Decision Support Systems (DSS) (2 hours)

    2.1. Visit the website www.computerworld.com/softwaretopics/ software/apps/story/0,10801,72327,00.html and read over the article about DSS. Also, refer to the figure above. A structured problem is characterized by having well-defined constraints and a definite right answer. An unstructured problem is often not well defined, and usually has no single "right" answer. Notice that the unstructured problems tend to belong to upper management, while the day to day transactions are more structured. Use these resources to create a business example of a structured problem and an example of an unstructured problem. . . .

    2.2. Visit the website www.prophix.com and glance over one of their case studies (listed in the area labeled Successes). Using your selected case study as an example, explain how Prophix, a DSS, can add value to a business (eight to ten sentences).

    2.3. Artificial intelligence is all about trying to make a computer act like a human being. In the future, many decisions currently made by people will be made by "artificial intelligence" systems. Visit www.bbc.co.uk/science/hottopics/ai/ for a look at AI topics. Briefly describe three topics you found interesting.

    2.4. AI introduces a new set of issues related to ethics. Read the story at www.wired.com/wired/archive/5.01/ffsupertoys_pr.html and list at least three ethical issues that could arise from the development of "super smart" computers.

    2.5. Glance over the article "How DNA Computers Will Work" at http://electronics.howstuffworks.com/dna-computer.htm. What are the advantages of DNA computers? Do you think super smart computers made with biological (instead of silicon) components will introduce even more ethical issues? Explain your answer.

    2.6. Go to www-ai.ijs.si/eliza/eliza.html and have a (free!) therapy session with one of the first AI systems developed. It simulates a therapist and tries to help you with your problems. . . . Make up a problem to see how the interaction proceeds. . . . Does Eliza pass the Turing Test—that is, could she make a human believe she was actually a human instead of a machine, in your opinion? Why or why not? . . . .

3. What's in the News? (1.5 hours). List several key points from each of these articles:

3.1. This first article is about CAPTCHAs. Have you ever signed up for a free e-mail account or used Ticketmaster and found that you were asked to describe symbols in the pictures before registering? You'll know why after reading this article. www .computerworld.com/securitytopics/security/story/0,10801,8 2025,00.html

3.2. The second article is about the use of AI in online auctions. www .computerworld.com/managementtopics/ebusiness/story/0,10 801,87391,00.html

3.3. The third is about intelligent agents, called "bots," and how they are used on the Internet. As before, the idea is to "skim" and not be put off by technical terms you don't understand; just take a quick look and try to summarize the key points. This experience should help you feel comfortable staying current with IT and the ways it affects business. www.computerworld. com/softwaretopics/software/story/0,10801,61539,00.html

4. Right-Brain Techniques to Tap into Your Unconsciousness (2 hours). In this assignment, you will have the option to keep the same challenge or create a new one, but please make it related to business. These intuitive techniques work best if you can find a challenge that you truly care about, since they require your subconscious to be involved. You will not be turning in your answers to these exercises in 4.1 and 4.2; instead you will just provide a write-up of your experience with the exercise.

4.1. *Thinkertoys* Chapter 22, "Chilling Out." It's a fact that you are more creative when your brain is producing alpha waves, and there are techniques for inducing an alpha-wave-producing state. . . . Read the chapter, and devote fifteen minutes to practicing any of the exercises of your choice. Describe briefly which exercises you tried and how well they seemed to work for you.

4.2. *Thinkertoys* Chapter 29, "DaVinci's Technique." Read through the chapter, then practice the technique in the blueprint on page 264. Again, please devote fifteen minutes to this exercise. Note that the drawings are doodles, not artistic sketches. In fact, thinking and drawing defeats the purpose. Like trying to see shapes in clouds, you are trying to see the inner workings of your mind by allowing it to unfocus and just doodle. Then try to see what shapes you might find in the doodles. Your subconscious mind communicates with symbols. When you are doodling and interpreting, you have a passageway between your conscious and subconscious mind. You don't need to turn these in, but please indicate that you have completed the exercise.

5. Self-Assessment (2 hours). Create a mind map on your computer that reflects and brings together what you have learned in this bundle. Your central concept should be "E-Business." . . . Like before, you should have at least 30 concepts and and at least 30 icons or symbols that reinforce these concepts. . . .

"A" Track Option (item 6): Only for students on the "A" Track

6. Show Your Learning (3 hours). This is basically the same assignment that you did in Learning Bundle 2. Demonstrate that you have invested at least three hours of your time in your software project. . . .

Examples as Options and Inspiration

I hope that this chapter has given you some sense of the variety of specs-graded course designs and the activities and assignments that can compose bundles and modules; the examples shown do not exhaust the possibilities. The bundles and modules that you develop need not be as elaborate as Kegley's, at least not if your course is face-to-face or hybrid because you can conduct many activities in class. But if you are teaching an online course, bundling many learning experiences and assessments and matching them to outcomes and grades represents a viable alternative to recording lectures, creating PowerPoint presentations, and developing online tests and interactive lessons. Let all the examples you have seen here serve to inspire your own ideas.

8

THE MOTIVATIONAL POWER
OF SPECS GRADING

It is reasonable to expect that specs grading might reduce students' motivation to learn and excel and encourage both them and their instructors to settle for less. After all, students need only pass tests and assignments to get through a course. But it does not seem to work that way, at least not when the pass standard is high. Recall that chapter 4 contains a number of testimonials about students being more motivated by faculty using specs grading or something very much like it. Davidson (2009) claims that her pass/fail system of grading assignments motivates her students to work harder and write more than traditional grading did. Mike Pulley (personal communication, December 3, 2012) reports that shifting his grading of the first draft of a team project from traditional to pass/fail has motivated his students to prepare much stronger drafts. Kunkel (2002) pushes his students to produce A-level work by giving no credit to anything less from them. Mastery learning, which is a pass/fail proposition, also generates higher quality student products than does traditional grading (Kulik, Kulik, & Bangert-Drowns, 1990). These are not flukes. I open this chapter by adding a few other testimonials and then consider why specs grading increases student motivation. I also examine other opportunities for adding motivational enhancements to a specs-graded course.

Additional Testimonials

Kathleen Kegley consistently reports that, whichever the course, her students have displayed greater motivation and more enthusiasm about their assignments than she previously saw using standard criterion-referenced grading (personal communication, October 7, 2011). So does Leff (n.d.). On average, his students have done three times as many assignments as have those of his departmental colleagues using a traditional grading system. His students complete more advanced assignments as well. Specifically, he finds:

> A third of the students in my CS3 (Assembler) completed A assignments. These involved difficult activities such as three-dimensional arrays, writing floating point emulators, and advanced input/output routines. They would be problems that couldn't be assigned to the whole class without intimidating a substantial number of the students. (Leff, n.d.)

Leff also claims that for some years he has let his students choose between his new grading system and the traditional one, and each year at least 90% of his students have chosen his new one.

Since switching to a system like specs grading, Hiller and Hietapelto (2001) believe that their students are more motivated for three good reasons: They display greater learning, they believe they have learned more, and they report feeling more motivated than when graded traditionally. Steve Davis (personal communication, November 4, 2011) used specs grading only for his last semester teaching management, after which he retired. But he found that his students seemed more motivated to learn and more interested in the course material and submitted higher quality work than when he used traditional grading. June Pilcher (personal communication, May 3, 2008, and November 14, 2011) has experienced similar results in her psychology classes. Most of her students have seemed more motivated and more interested in the material. With specs grading, she changed practically all her assessment instruments, replacing standard exams with new and totally different homework assignments, notably longer and more open-ended. So she has not been in a position to judge changes in the quality of student work. She has spent more time grading these assignments than the standard tests she used to rely on, but she now enjoys the process more.

The pressing question is, Why should students be more motivated to learn, more interested in the material, and apparently more willing to work in a specs-graded course? Is it just the threat of failure? No doubt that contributes. Pass/fail grading raises the stakes for any assessment. Reading and following the directions, understanding the problem, addressing the question, and completing the task are more important and consequential than they are when partial credit can save the day. Having specs-graded his students' first drafts of their service-learning project reports in 15 sections of his technical writing course over three semesters, Pulley summed up the success of the new system this way:

> What I discovered was that it achieved my goal of motivating students. Despite the low points value for the rough draft, I've noticed that students work harder when they hear that anything less than a perfect assignment will result in the grade of zero or F. . . . They now have a draft that they can manage to revise adequately in those last two weeks. In the end, the quality of the final projects went up and the final grades on the final projects . . . are higher—so, it's like a win-win for everyone. My service-learning clients . . . are happier with the final projects and more apt to use them in their businesses and organizations—in the real world. The students are happier because they have higher grades and see their work getting used for real in the real world, and I'm happier because I managed to motivate my students—at least motivate them to a level beyond what I had been able to do previously on this one assignment. (personal communication, April 24, 2014)

But pass/fail grading cannot account for students' greater interest in the material. The next section discusses theories of motivation that clarify why specs grading stimulates *intrinsic* motivation, which encompasses interest in the material, as well as the desire to excel.

Motivating Features of Specs Grading

There are five relevant theories of motivation that apply to students: self-efficacy, expectancy-value of goal achievement, goal orientation (performance versus learning), self-determination, and goal setting. They all have hundreds if not thousands of studies to support them.

The theories of self-efficacy and expectancy-value of goal achievement are very similar in that both posit that the motivation to achieve varies directly with a person's expectation of success in achieving the goal, and both rest this expectation on the person's belief that he knows *how* to attain that goal and feels capable of doing it (Bandura, 1977, 1997; Wigfield & Eccles, 2000). Why pour energy into pursuing something one is unlikely to obtain? A student's confidence in achieving a goal may stem from his history of successes, the resources provided to achieve, or the clarity with which the expectations are laid out. But also critical is his belief in an *internal* locus of control, meaning that he sees himself in control of his life outcomes and attributes them to his own efforts and determination. When the element of free choice and volition in goal selection accompanies an internal locus of control, a student believes he can *choose* to aspire to whatever level of achievement he is willing to put in the time and effort toward.

By contrast, students who subscribe to an *external* locus of control perceive that outside forces—typically the instructor, the students' inborn and immutable abilities, or fate—determine their academic outcomes, and they therefore take little or no responsibility for them, especially their failures. They make statements to an instructor such as "*You* gave me a C," "I can't do math," and "You should be making this material easy for me to learn." They do not think that they should have to persist and expend effort to learn, and they are often speaking from their K–12 experience where they received As for doing very little work. When such students come to college expecting to be held to the same low standards, and they discover the rules have changed, their sense of self-efficacy and the expectancy-value of their academic goals slip—that is, they no longer expect success because of forces they view as beyond their control—and their motivation to learn correspondingly drops.

According to goal orientation theory, a learning orientation generates stronger motivation to learn than a performance orientation. When adopting the former, students willingly practice new skills, monitor their learning, and undergo assessments, realizing that they can use these experiences as vehicles for feedback and learning and will naturally start out making mistakes and hitting walls. Because they are willing to embrace challenges and risks, they not only achieve mastery over time but also produce more creative work. By contrast, a performance orientation aims not to learn and master abilities but to appear competent to others, gain their praise, and avoid their criticism. Performance-oriented students choose to avoid risk and error. They do not want to look "stupid" to their instructors or peers, so they do whatever they think is necessary to put on a good performance. They care desperately about their grades and may very well get excellent ones, but they will do so by taking the easier courses; turning in conventional work; and relying on the safer study strategies, which in many cases is memorizing the material, which is what they learned to do in their early schooling. They avoid any level of assessment at which they may fail, which is their greatest fear (Dweck & Leggett, 1988; Elliott & Dweck, 1988).

Self-determination theory hypothesizes that the motivation to achieve derives from people's need to grow and gain fulfillment—that is, to acquire new knowledge and skills, to become more independent, and to live through new experiences. For students, a sense of growth and gratification depends on their belief that they have these qualities: (a) competence, by learning and mastering skills and tasks; (b) connection or relatedness, by feeling attached to others and affiliated with a social group; and (c) autonomy, by experiencing control over their own goals, behaviors, and outcomes (Deci & Ryan, 1985). Because of the drive for autonomy, freely choosing a goal enhances its value and the motivation to pursue it.

Finally, goal-setting theory (Locke & Latham, 1990) posits that just setting a goal heightens a student's motivation to achieve it, which in turn enhances the effort, strategic thinking, performance, and persistence that she puts toward achieving that goal. The conditions for making this happen are quite simple. A student has to choose the goal freely, see it as specific and measurable, get feedback on her progress toward it, and perceive it as challenging but attainable. This last condition is especially salient for our purposes. In fact, as the difficulty of the goal rises, a person's effort and performance steadily increases. As a goal, a high grade in a specs-graded course meets all the theory's conditions for driving this relationship: It is freely chosen (see the next section), specific, measurable, and challenging but attainable, and students get feedback on their progress toward it. This theory has been the most heavily researched and most widely implemented perspective in industrial and organizational psychology for the past 50 years (Redmond & Perrin, 2014).

All these theories shed light on why specs grading augments motivation. From the theories of self-efficacy and expectancy-value of goal achievement, we know that clear expectations—a crucial element of specs grading—raise a student's confidence in her ability to attain a goal and reinforce her belief in an internal locus of control. When she knows what she has to do to meet the specs of the work, she feels in control of her academic outcomes (Fraser, 1990). Consequently, she is willing to put forth more effort toward a goal (Polczynski & Shirland, 1977). This sense of control strengthens her perceived autonomy, which bolsters her self-determination.

This greater sense of agency and control also supports a learning orientation. Students only have to make sure their work meets the specs. Beyond that, they should have little worry or stress about their performance, so they can afford to focus more on their learning. Given the clear expectations for their work, they should feel quite capable of achieving them (Fraser, 1990). They should also feel comfortable taking risks within the parameters of the specs.

In addition, the high standards to which specs grading holds students enhances their sense of self-efficacy, competency, and achievement once they reach their goal. In fact, communicating high expectations is one of Chickering and Gamson's (1987) seven principles for good practice in undergraduate education. They explain the power of high expectations this way:

> Expect more and you will get more. High expectations are important for everyone—for the poorly prepared, for those unwilling to exert themselves, and for the bright and well motivated. Expecting students to perform well

becomes a self-fulfilling prophecy when teachers and institutions hold high
expectations for themselves and make extra efforts. (p. 5)

In other words, many students are quite capable of doing more and doing
better than what we may ask them to do. The National Survey of Student
Engagement (2013) reports that about 55% of first-year students and 61%
of seniors strongly agree that their courses have challenged them to do their
best work. In addition, high standards raise the difficulty level of a goal. Goal-
setting theory tells us that as long as the goal is feasible, greater challenge
increases students' effort, strategic thinking, performance, and persistence to
achieve that goal.

Specs grading allows for considerable choice, as explored in the next
section. Consistent with goal-setting theory, it even lets students select
the workload and grade they wish to pursue. This is a topic that we have
not addressed in any depth before now. Yet it is important because when
students can choose their grade, the way they will be assessed, the topic of
their project, or their modality of expression, their autonomy enhances the
value of whatever they select and their motivation to perform the task well
(Fraser, 1990). They perceive choice as a way to meet their needs and interests (Chyung, 2007).

Arenas of Choice and Control

Let's now home in on the opportunities for choice and control that specs
grading permits.

Choice of Grade and Accompanying Workload

Letting students choose their grade in advance, which bundles and modules allow, empowers students to take responsibility for their own academic
results and assume control over their own time and energy. They are not only
choosing a grade but also the amount and challenge of the work they will do
for a course, and we should respect those choices. If a student opts for a C or
a D, she presumably has her reasons, and she can leave the course without a
sense of failure. Still, we should encourage all students to aim high and not
let a lack of confidence lower the aspirations of those not accustomed to academic success (Gabriel, 2008).

Virtually all the courses we examined in the last chapter provide that
choice. So do those taught by Waldenberger (2012), Jeffrey Appling, Steve
Stevenson, and Wayne Stewart, as well as all of those developed by Kegley
and Pilcher. Leff (n.d.) gives his students their choice of easier or more

difficult assignments for different grades. In Kunkel's (2002) courses, choice is more limited. Because students receive a final grade based on the proportion of their work that merits an A, they can choose to accept a lower grade only by not revising their lesser work. Students have similar choices in Davidson's (2009) classes. Venditti (2010), Pulley, and Cynthia Pury do not grant choices, but they are using specs grading in more restricted ways.

Choice of Token Use

Incorporating a token economy into your course, as have Kegley, Pilcher, and Terry, adds whole new dimensions of choices and trade-offs while giving students more flexible control of their time. Of course, we should encourage students to keep their tokens by rewarding them for doing so. But they should decide for themselves whether they want to give up a token for a 24-hour extension or a missed class or risk having to give one up for not doing their best work the first time. Should they conserve their tokens for truly rainy days or a reward at the end of the term? Should they try to earn more tokens by submitting some assignments early? Every student has to consider and select among the options we allow many times during the term—and live with the consequences.

Choice of Assignments

Providing alternative ways to satisfy assignments not only builds motivation but also reduces grade anxiety and grade-grubbing (Svinicki, 2004). The research-based courses described in chapter 7—one combining research with engagement and the other combining research with fieldwork—offer the broadest and most flexible selection of assignments. Recall that Janice Lanham's Health Promotion, Physical Activity, and Obesity Prevention in Children, Adolescents, and Teenagers gives students vying for a B a choice of any two out of 10 tasks within the project and those aiming for an A a choice of any four (personal communication, August 26, 2011). The tasks include developing a case scenario, compiling data, designing an online survey, and producing a podcast presentation. Similarly, Will Mayo, Susan Pope, and Jennifer Goree's course, Healthy Communities Initiative, asks students pursuing a B to do two tasks and those desiring an A to do four tasks from a list of eight, which includes attending three campus programs related to health and wellness, helping a campus unit with administering a survey, and interviewing a faculty member who conducts health-related research.

Choice of Various Aspects of Assignments: Topics, Modalities, and Work Settings

We first explored Pilcher's Advanced Physiological Psychology course in chapter 3 as an example of a system that bases higher grades on jumping both more hurdles and higher hurdles. But it also illustrates ways to provide students with options within assignments. For instance, for their final project, Pilcher lets students choose any brain-behavior topic and explain to an audience why and how the human brain operates the way it does to impact a specific behavior. Students can select either to work alone or to form a team of any number for this project. She just warns them that each team must handle its own internal problems, such as voting off slackers or sandbaggers. Adding a creative dimension, she allows them to choose the modality of expression. To provide specs without restricting their imaginations, she furnishes many examples of possible individual projects (e.g., scripting and filming a half-hour documentary like those on PBS or the Discovery Channel; producing a series of public-service TV commercials totaling 30 minutes; developing a set of five informational brochures, each about four pages, with references, for first-year students; writing a well-referenced research proposal of 15–20 pages requesting funding) and team projects (dramatizing a well-documented debate or an educational play of about a half hour). But Pilcher means these ideas only as examples. Students can create something else if they prefer as long as she approves the plan in advance (personal communication, May 3, 2008).

Choice of Submission Deadlines

You might not consider this an entirely attractive range of options, but Leff (n.d.) does let his computer science students decide when to hand in assignments. Being on time rewards students with a lighter workload, whereas being late costs them time and effort, whether they are aiming for an A, a B, or a C. The following is how he structures his system:

- On-time submission—6 activities required

    C requirements: 6 of the easiest activities
    B requirements: 6 somewhat more difficult activities
    A requirements: 6 challenging activities

- Slightly late submission—8 activities required

    C requirements: 8 of the easiest activities
    B requirements: 8 somewhat more difficult activities
    A requirements: 8 challenging activities

- Very late submission—12 activities required

  C requirements: 12 of the easiest activities
  B requirements: 12 somewhat more difficult activities
  A requirements: 12 challenging activities

Of course, Leff is incentivizing being on time and not procrastinating.

Other Arenas of Choice and Control Within a Point System

If you use a point system, you can set it up to give your students even more choices. For instance, you can develop a menu of assessments, as did the instructors of the two previously discussed research-focused courses. But in a point system, each menu option is worth a certain number of points, and students can choose assignments and tests from the menu as they work toward the point total they hope to earn for a given grade. Admittedly, this involves considerable work for you—both in developing an extensive menu on the front end and in keeping track of each student's point accumulation during the course (Hiller & Hietapelto, 2001). This consumes more time than just noting whether students have done two, four, or no assignments from a list of eight or nine.

Some faculty have experimented with letting students choose the percentage weight for each assignment and test—in other words, letting them determine the distribution of points across assignments and tests—within certain limits (Dobrow, Smith, & Posner, 2011; Hiller & Hietapelto, 2001; Vander Schee, 2009; Warrington, Hietapelto, & Joyce, 2003). This means, of course, that you have a different point structure for each student, which could become overwhelming in a medium to large class. Neither Dobrow et al. nor Vander Schee detected any noticeable differences in their final grade distributions from the ones they obtained using traditional criteria-referenced grading. Hiller and Hietapelto's students achieved higher grades than those in previous traditionally graded classes, but the researchers found that the students learned more as well. An uptick in grades coupled with a comparable increase in learning is not grade inflation.

Students' Choice of Outcomes

Hiller and Hietapelto (2001) advocate allowing students to select their own learning goals or outcomes. Although this idea may motivate students, it may or may not be feasible in courses that have outcomes built into them. Ask yourself this: What outcomes *must* the students in your course achieve in order for your program, curriculum, or institution to be accredited or meet some other important requirement? If you are bundling assessments, then achieving these essential outcomes should define the requirements for the lowest passing grade in the course (usually a C or D). If you are using a point system, then you must structure your assessments so that students who pass the course will have successfully completed at least one assessment in all the required outcomes. Students can then choose from among additional outcomes.

Leff (n.d.) uses a point system in a course that has required learning goals, and he has developed a strategy to ensure his passing students can meet them. He defines several "genres" of points in which each genre represents one of the educational goals (content mastery or cognitive skills) or performance goals (amount of work) that the department requires in that course. In Leff's area, one major performance goal is writing a minimal number of lines of code. So he defines a genre for each essential piece of content mastery or skill (e.g., bit-diddling and arrays) and another for lines of code. Each assessment is worth so many points toward meeting one or more educational goals and one or more performance goals, and he sets the minimum number of points in each genre that students must accumulate to earn a passing grade in the course. This minimum number ensures that all passing students have done an acceptable job on at least one assessment of every required educational and performance goal.

Specs Grading, Choice, and Student Satisfaction

At the beginning of this chapter, we heard from faculty who have found that using specs grading or something like it has enhanced their students' motivation to learn and produce better work. Giving students more choice and control has had other positive impacts as well.

Gibbs (Rhem, 2011) claims that her students show higher engagement and more ambition. Both Davis (personal communication, November 4, 2011) and Pilcher (personal communication, May 3, 2008; November 14, 2011) report that their students demonstrate more interest in the course material and register fewer grading protests. According to Pilcher, the drop in grading complaints stems from their "know[ing] every step of the way what they are doing to meet the requirements for each grade category." Janet Craig (personal communication, November 7, 2011) notes that her students complain less about the amount of work required for the course, which she explains this way: "Control and responsibility shifted to the students. [It has been] up to them to decide how much work they wanted to do." Just giving students control over weighting their assignments and tests may enhance student interest in the material and in taking more courses in the same content area (Dobrow et al., 2011). Hiller and Hietapelto (2001), Craig, Leff, and

Pilcher claim that their students' satisfaction with specs-graded courses has been high and that most students prefer specs grading to traditional grading; Davis did not find this in his course. Although students being pleased by something we do is a pleasant outcome, it is not among our criteria for evaluating a grading system.

9

DEVELOPING A COURSE
WITH SPECS GRADING

This chapter provides detailed directions for and advice to faculty who wish to implement the specs grading strategy in their courses. The same principles of course design apply across face-to-face, online, and hybrid environments. The key topics addressed here are how to design a "pure" specs grading course and what you might call a "synthetic" course, which uses both specs and traditional grading. Although the latter type does not yield all the benefits of specs grading, it is sometimes necessary to accommodate institutional requirements. Faculty may also prefer to start small with this new grading system and ease into it. In addition, because students probably have not seen anything like specs grading in their educational lives, the chapter explains how to introduce this new grading system to them. But first let's look at why and how some of the pioneering faculty we featured in chapters 3, 4, and 7 made the transition.

Why Others Did It

Faculty give a wide range of reasons for shifting to specs grading. Management professor Janis Miller (personal communication, April 15, 2014) cites the following: It rewards students on the basis of their willingness to work; it allows students who are not great test takers, especially those for whom English is a second language, to earn an A; it enabled her to eliminate attendance requirements for students vying for less than a B, thus drastically reducing classroom incivilities and disruptions; and it allowed her to reserve the final project for the A-bound students. This final project had yielded some very disappointing and difficult-to-grade products in the past. Now she only has to grade high-quality ones. For computer science professor Steve Stevenson (personal communication, April 15, 2014), specs grading made sense for his problem-based field. His students write programs and a reflective essay for the final exam, which are well suited for pass/fail assessment. He claims that the only thing he left behind was "a hundred years of mathematics instruction of boring definition-theorem-proof." Chemistry professor Jeffrey Appling (personal communication, April 16, 2014) was attracted to specs grading because of its simplicity and the fact that it gets rid of grade-grubbing. Psychology professor Cynthia Pury (personal communication, April 22, 2014) embraced it to motivate her research methods students to complete their Institutional Review Board (IRB) proposal on time. Mike Pulley (personal communication, April 24, 2014) adopted it for a similar reason: to motivate his technical writing students to start drafting their service-learning project early and do a good job on the first draft. Nursing professor Janice Lanham (personal communication, April 22, 2014) appreciated the flexible control it gives students over the quantity and quality of their course work and found that students indeed like this control.

All of these faculty found integrating and implementing specs grading in their courses quite easy. Lanham sought advice from a colleague already using the system and introduced it first in her small classes. At first, Miller found it difficult to allow those who scored only 70% on the tests to earn an A, but she says this aspect of her grading system has served both her and her students well. She also feels she now allocates her grading time more sensibly, devoting the bulk of it to the more motivated students who are most interested in her feedback. While Stevenson did not have to adopt any new assumptions, Appling found he had to discard his assumption that B students would not do A-level work, because some of them indeed rose to the opportunity. But Pury had to adjust her mind-set in the other direction: to be willing to fail a student for not meeting the IRB proposal deadline. She had to accept that she could no longer play "supernice, superunderstanding instructor." However, she developed a plan for students' legitimate excuses, such as being hospitalized the week before the deadline. Pulley also had to assume that he could "muster the courage" to fail students on their first drafts and that students would accept a fail if they merited it. On the other hand, he says he abandoned his rigid notion that there was only one way to grade students. For Lanham, the major change involved giving up her primary control over grades and sharing it with her students. She also had to revise her assignments to reflect the final grade levels (A, B, C, etc.). Like her, Stevenson also adopted a more collaborative approach to teaching and now encourages student participation in developing the syllabus and the course. On the first day, he asks his class, "What do you think you should know about the subject?"

An instructor cannot design bundles or modules without first identifying the cognitive level(s) of their component assignments and the specific outcomes that these assignments assess. So specs grading should make faculty more explicit about these levels and outcomes. Both Stevenson and Appling already articulated sound outcomes aimed for specific, high cognitive levels. But Lanham found herself focusing more explicitly on her learning outcomes and the level of thinking they required as a result of her transitioning to specs grading. While Pulley has relied on a point system instead of bundles or modules, specs grading just one assignment induced him to add detail to his learning outcomes and grading criteria. The new system sensitized Miller to the fact that her C students had not engaged in high-level thinking in the past, whereas her A students consistently had.

Designing a Pure Specs Course

In a pure specs type of course, you grade all student work pass/fail and either bundle your assessments or assign a point value to each individual assessment. The first step is to examine your current assessments and accompanying grading rubrics. Can you furnish a set of clear specifications to describe what you want your students to do? The highest and second highest levels of your rubric may supply at least some of the criteria you seek. You might find it best to modify or revise one or more assignments to ensure that you can develop unambiguous specs for them. Also consider adding a required minimum length and maybe even a maximum length, as well as the number of hours (or minutes) that you think students will need to complete the assignment.

The second step is to decide how to assign course grades. Let's say you would like to bundle your assessments and match each bundle to the final grade:

- To receive an A in the course, the student must complete the A module.
- To receive a B in the course, the student must complete the B module.

- To receive a C in the course, the student must complete the C module.
- To receive a D in the course, the student must complete the D module.

It would entail extra work to develop entirely different assessments for each grade. And what if a student completes the C-level work by the deadline and then wants to do the B-level work? So consider breaking the A bundle into four modular components, such that the first module is the same work required to earn a D in the course; the first and second modules are required to earn a C in the course; the first, second, and third modules are required to earn a B in the course; and all four modules are required to earn an A. As shown in Figure 9.1, you can determine final grades with this simple scheme:

- To receive an A in the course, the student must complete levels 1, 2, 3, and 4.
- To receive a B in the course, the student must complete levels 1, 2, and 3.
- To receive a C in the course, the student must complete levels 1 and 2.
- To receive a D in the course, the student must complete level 1.
- The student will receive an F in the course for not completing level 1.

This approach allows you to set successive deadlines for the work at the ascending levels during the course, thereby spreading out your grading duties and evaluating the same body of work after each deadline. It also furnishes students who are pursuing an A with a series of deadlines to help them pace

Figure 9.1.   Simple Specs Grading Scheme With Course Grades Assigned Based on Completion of Modules

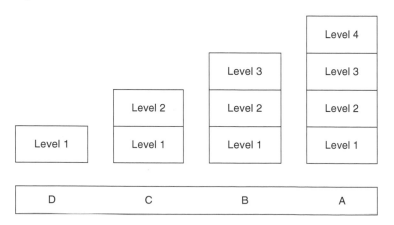

their efforts and gives all students decision points during the course to determine whether or not they want to continue to the next level. This is one of the many choice junctures that can enhance students' intrinsic motivation.

Alternatively, you can create a collection of bundles and allow students to choose which and how many of the bundles to complete. Let's say that you develop a total of eight bundles. Your grading scheme might look like this:

- To receive an A in the course, the student must complete any 7 of the 8 bundles.
- To receive a B in the course, the student must complete any 6 of the 8 bundles.
- To receive a C in the course, the student must complete any 5 of the 8 bundles.
- To receive a D in the course, the student must complete any 4 of the 8 bundles.
- Completing fewer than 4 bundles will result in an F in the course.

Although this approach allows for more student choice, it can make it difficult for you to guarantee that your students are achieving specific learning outcomes unless each bundle assesses the same outcomes. Of course, if your accrediting agency and the curriculum do not require your course to address specific outcomes, you can design your bundles around different outcomes and let your students choose their outcomes. Another potentially tricky issue will be staggering the deadlines for the different bundles to avoid a grading avalanche at the end of the term.

An alternative to bundles or modules is the point system—that is, basing final grades on the number of points that each student accumulates across various quizzes, tests, and assignments during the course, all of which are graded pass/fail. As explained in chapter 6, this system has its weaknesses. Point totals tend not to correspond to outcomes achieved, students may not select their target grade in advance, and offering many separate assessments can make the grading system complicated. On the other hand, it can be designed to offer students numerous choices of assessments.

Designing a Synthetic Grading Course

The pure specs grading approach may be most beneficial, but some faculty may find the change disorienting and prefer to ease into the new system or selectively use components of it. In this case, you might envision the course design task as a hierarchy of options. The two grading systems can be used in combination to evaluate (a) student performance on different assessment instruments, (b) different levels of student performance on an assessment instrument, (c) student performance on rubric criteria, and (d) student performance on different items within an assessment instrument. A synthetic option may appeal especially to faculty who rely on objective tests to determine course grades.

Assessment Instruments

Faculty can apply specs grading selectively—for example, only on the assessment instruments required to earn an A in the course, or only on the instruments required to earn an A or a B, or only on the instruments required to earn a C or above. Faculty can apply specs grading in the other direction as well, using it only on the assessment instruments required to earn one of the lower grades and reserving traditional grading to determine the higher grades.

One simple synthetic grading scheme relies on a standard commonly used for professional certification. For example, passing may require a score of 70% or higher on a traditional exam, while failing results from any score lower than 70%. In the following example, the passing grade of C relies on traditional grading and higher grades on specs grading:

- To receive a C in the course, the student must have a total average score of 70% or higher on all the exams.
- To receive a B in the course, the student must meet the requirements for a C, plus complete Module B.
- To receive an A in the course, the student must meet the requirements for a B, plus complete Module A.

Within this structure, students self-select to do more or less work, giving you more time to coach those most motivated to learn.

Pury uses a different but equally simple synthetic grading framework in her undergraduate methodology course. To pass the course, students must submit an acceptable proposal for an independent research project to the campus IRB. The hard-and-fast due date is just before the deadline for dropping a course, which allows students who are not keeping up with the course to withdraw rather than get an F. Beyond this required, on-time proposal, Pury uses a traditional system to determine all the other grades: An A requires earning at least 90% of the available points, a B requires earning at least 80%, and so on. Since instituting the on-time proposal requirement, she has not had to fail anyone or give an "Incomplete." Similarly, Pulley grades only one of his writing assignments pass/fail, the first draft of the major team project. Both he and Pury selected the assignment they did because previously so many of their students did not take it seriously enough.

An online course variation of this grading scheme is to use nonproctored exams for the minimal C-level assessment, then specs grading to assess B- and A-level assignments. Or, if it is possible, an instructor might require students to take a proctored exam to vie for the A or B course grades. Either option reduces the faculty workload.

Performance Level

Rather than using a different grading system for different assessment instruments, you can use both systems together in evaluating a single major assessment instrument. For example, a paper, project, or portfolio can earn a B by meeting all bottom-line standards and an A by exceeding those standards in the professional judgment of the instructor. In other words, products receive a B or lower according to the specs grading system and higher grades according to the traditional system.

Rhetoric professor Jeffrey M. Ringer has used this approach to determine portfolio (and ultimately course) grades. He assembled a bundle of largely behavioral conditions for students to get a B: a good attendance and on-time arrival record, completion of writing notebooks (free writes and reading responses), cooperative team behavior, submission of a complete portfolio, and specific writing assignments that meet certain standards. Failing to meet all these conditions would result in a C or an F. Ringer gave the portfolios higher grades (A, A-, and B+) based on the quality of the work. English professor Risa Applegarth (cited in Elbow, 2009) grades her students' portfolios using a very similar system. She reserves grades higher than a B for portfolios that exhibit "exceptionally strong" writing.

For his 20th Century U.S. Foreign Policy course, political science professor Michael J. Strada anchored his system in the minimal work requirements for earning a C in the course: completing a number of papers that earn a passing grade (revisions allowed on some of them), passing two tests, and being absent from no more than three classes. From this baseline, he set the lower grades: a D for failing to complete any one of the minimum requirements and an F for failing to complete any two of these requirements. For both the B and A grades, students had to complete all the minimum work requirements plus additional papers, the short one graded pass/fail and the long one graded on traditional quality criteria. The pass/fail paper (a position paper) had a required length of 500 words for a B and 1,000 words for an A. The traditionally graded paper (a research paper) also had length requirements, with the A paper having to be at least twice as long as the B paper. In addition, the A paper had to reflect all the positive qualities of the B paper plus many more that demonstrated higher-order thinking skills, greater depth, and more thorough research.

Assessment Criteria

A synthetic grading schema based on assessment criteria presumes that the instructor is using an analytical rubric to grade a student product. What is graded pass/fail is the product's quality *on each criterion* in the rubric. Recall the description in chapter 4 of how Venditti (2010) assesses his public-speaking students' portfolios. He grades these capstone assignments satisfactory/unsatisfactory (25 or 0 points) on each of four criteria: completeness (all required items submitted), professionalism, writing quality, and the length and punctuality of the oral presentation. Although this allows students to hand in substandard work on one criterion or another, the consequences are not trivial; they lose one fourth of the possible points for each criterion on which their portfolio falls short.

Assessment Items

Perhaps the easiest way to include pass/fail grading in the traditional point-based system is to incorporate some test or homework items—perhaps short-answer questions, short essays, or an extra-credit problem—that are evaluated on a pass/fail basis. Although these microlevel assessments do not reap many of the specifications grading benefits, they can serve as an entry point for developing a pure course incrementally.

For example, you might begin by including some specs-graded sections within a traditionally graded exam, such as a 10-point essay or a 25-point application problem. Over a few terms, you should become more familiar and comfortable with the approach.

Introducing Students to Specs Grading

Though students tend to embrace specs grading quickly, the pass/fail scheme can be unsettling for some, especially when they realize that partial credit is no longer possible. For example, they may become suspicious of the instructor's motives or overly anxious about the likelihood of their success. At the other extreme, some students may assume that the absence of partial credit means that everyone will automatically pass regardless of the quality of his or her work.

Faculty may have to defend their no-partial-credit policy. If so, they can point to Chickering and Gamson's (1987) principle for good practice in undergraduate education that recommends holding students to high expectations. They can also refer to the startling findings in Arum and Roksa's *Academically Adrift* (2011) indicating that 36% of students showed no significant progress in their learning over four years, and that those who did improve made only modest gains, according to their Collegiate Learning Assessment (CLA) scores. Tinto (n.d.) calls high faculty expectations a condition for student success. He cites a finding from the National Survey of Student Engagement (2013) that first-year students spend much less out-of-class time on their course work than the recommended three hours for each hour in class. This result was confirmed by Babcock and Marks's (2011) comparative examination of today's students' study time versus that of students 50 years ago, whether or not they were also employed. Tinto believes that instructors simply do not expect enough of them, and some students concur. Only 55% of first-year students and 61% of seniors strongly agree that their courses have challenged them to do their best work (National Survey of Student Engagement, 2013). We still have a way to go before all students feel that we expect them to produce the best.

Faculty should inform their students of the key role that high expectations play in their academic success and admit that instructors have failed to maintain the rigorous standards that students can and should rise to.

To help all students begin a specs-graded course with a constructive mindset, it is important to introduce the rationale for the structure of the course and the grading system. In particular, explaining the concept of andragogy or adult-based learning theory (Forrest & Peterson, 2008; Knowles, 1975, 1980, 1984, 1986) helps them understand and buy into the approach. For example, a basic principle, such as adults preferring to have some choice in their learning experience and learning best in a safe yet challenging environment, will usually resonate with students. So do comparisons with real-world certifications, such as the common practice of grading professional licensing exams (nursing, medical, and bar exams) pass/fail.

In addition to an oral explanation, the syllabus should carry a written statement about andragogy. After telling her students that they will be actively involved in their own learning, June Pilcher includes this passage in her Health Psychology and Advanced Physiological Psychology syllabus:

> We will do this through implementing adult-based learning theory or "andragogy." Andragogy maintains that adults learn best when they have a flexible but challenging learning environment. We will create a positive but challenging learning environment in this course. Instead of tests, there will be a variety of assignments from which each student can choose how much to do in order to get the grade she or he wishes. This will allow students to direct their learning in this course in the manner that best suits their learning objectives.

In her Bioinformatics course, Kathleen Kegley puts this explanation in the syllabus:

Adult-based learning theory, or "andragogy," states that adults learn best in a low-threat, interesting, and challenging environment. The area of bio-informatics certainly offers an interesting challenge, and the design of the course structure embraces the low-threat component of andragogy. There are no traditional exams, and the open-ended assignments allow students to pursue tasks in a manner customized to individual needs and interests.

In her syllabi for her online courses, Kegley links certain features of her course to adult-based learning theory:

> You will find examples of this theory throughout the course design, as it forms the basis for the online delivery, the grading scheme, the relatively few deadlines, and the choices you are given to work on topics and problems that are related to your own interests, background, and career goals. The grading is "safe" in that each module is graded either pass or fail, and the require-ments for a pass are clearly stated. Typically incomplete or disrespectful work justifies a "fail." It is easy for students to tell whether their work is complete, done in good faith, and consonant with the intended learning outcome.

Another effective approach is first to explain the concept of andragogy and then to give students a short written assignment due within the first week of class that asks them to describe several ways that the course embraces it. Nat-urally, this assignment should be graded pass/fail, and students should merit a pass for any reasonable answer (you may want to specify a certain length). This experience helps students get acquainted and comfortable with specs grading. You may then elect to compile their answers and present them to the entire class. Kegley has found this assignment effective in engaging students and building their understanding and appreciation of this new approach. She has also used it to inquire whether they have any specific concerns or ques-tions, thus prompting them to voice anything they might otherwise keep to themselves.

Miller (personal communication, April 15, 2014) explains specs grading with an analogy, showing her class pictures of water sports: waterskiing to represent the C requirements of the course, which are broad but not deep; snorkeling to represent the B requirements, which are deeper and not so broad; and scuba diving to represent the in-depth project that an A addi-tionally requires. Her explanation also suggests the learning outcomes at the different grade levels.

Giving students one or more tokens or otherwise permitting them one or two opportunities to revise or drop substandard work reinforces the safety of the learning environment. These safety-net mechanisms should also be explained in the syllabus, along with how they support andragogy. After all, adult life can be complex and difficult to control, and it can get in the way of being able to submit satisfactory work on time every time.

Making the Transition

As faculty experience bears out, it is not difficult to transition to specs grading. Most assignments should be readily adaptable to setting specs for a satisfactory performance, and many course features—assessment instruments, performance levels, assessment criteria, and assessment items—can easily incorporate features of both traditional and specs grading. For those who wish to transform their traditionally graded course to a pure specs-graded one, Table 9.1 provides guidance on how to adapt existing course components.

The final chapter revisits the criteria laid out at the beginning of the book for evaluating a grading system and summarizes how specs grading measures up.

TABLE 9.1.

Making the Transition From Traditional to Specs Grading

Traditional Grading	Adapted to Specs Grading
Standard grading policy in syllabus needing little or no explanation or justification, with more points leading to a higher course grade	Explain and "sell" specs grading to students, referring to the relationship between high expectations and student success, the need for greater rigor, the concept of andragogy, the effectiveness of a safe yet challenging environment, pass/fail practices in licensing exams and employment, and any meaningful analogy.
	Emphasize the choice and control they will have over their course grade; workload; token use; and possibly other aspects of the course, such as their assignments and the outcomes they will achieve (see chapter 8).

(*Continues*)

TABLE 9.1.
Making the Transition From Traditional to Specs Grading (Continued)

Traditional Grading	Adapted to Specs Grading
Series of assignments and tests over the term required of all students, usually culminating in a major challenging assignment late in the term Students required to attend all classes and/or participate in all online class forums	Identify the cognitive level(s) of all assignments and tests and the specific outcomes they assess (except those only for reading compliance). Redesign existing assignments and tests as needed. Group the assignments and tests into three or four bundles or modules that entail different amounts of work (more hurdles) and/or different levels of academic challenge (higher hurdles, higher cognitive level). Associate each bundle/module with a course grade, awarding higher grades for more work and/or higher academic challenge. Make the major challenging assignment a requirement only for an A. Consider allowing students some choice over assignments, features of assignments, due dates, and the like. Set deadlines for completion of C and D bundles/modules after the middle but before the end of the term.
No clear relationship between course grades and outcomes achievement False appearance that all students have attained all the learning outcomes by the end of the course	Explicitly link each bundle/module with the outcome(s) that students will demonstrate by successfully completing it.

(Continues)

TABLE 9.1.

Making the Transition From Traditional to Specs Grading (Continued)

Traditional Grading	Adapted to Specs Grading
Multilevel rubrics to assess assignments and essay tests	Develop specs from the top one or two levels of the traditional rubrics. Elaborate the specs, making them as specific and unambiguous as possible. Lay out a formula or template for a complex assignment or essay test.
Partial credit	Grade all assignments and tests pass/fail, credit/no credit, satisfactory/unsatisfactory against the specs. Be willing to return work as unacceptable/no credit to a student.
Opportunities to revise work for a higher grade or more points	Allow students to exchange a token for the opportunity to revise unsatisfactory work *or* allow them to revise only the first assignment *or* stipulate that if students submit drafts for instructor and/or peer feedback and they do not meet certain specs, they will receive no credit or feedback.
Late work policies	Allow students to exchange a token for a 24-hour extension.

10

AN EVALUATION OF SPECS GRADING

L et's review the distinguishing features, or specs, of specs grading in its pure form:

- Students are graded pass/fail on individual assignments and tests or on bundles or modules of assignments and tests.
- Instructors provide very clear, detailed specifications (specs)—even models if necessary—for what constitutes a passing (acceptable/ satisfactory) piece of work.
- Specs reflect the standards of B-level or better work.
- Students are allowed at least one opportunity to revise an unacceptable piece of work, or start the course with a limited number of tokens that they can exchange to revise or drop unacceptable work or to submit work late.
- Bundles and modules that earn higher course grades require students to demonstrate mastery of more skills and content, more advanced/ complex skills and content, or both.
- Bundles and modules are tied to the learning outcomes of the course or the program. Students will not necessarily achieve all the possible outcomes, but their course grade will indicate which ones they have and have not achieved. (Using a point system with specs grading

compromises the relationship between grades and outcomes, but other benefits of the system still apply.)

As we have examined the various features of specs grading throughout this book, we have been evaluating it against the criteria for grading systems we set up in chapter 1. Recall that the system we currently use did not stack up very well, and it has had many decades to prove its worth. Here we summarize our assessments, holding to the assumption that specs grading is implemented completely and correctly. In this case, specs grading achieves the purposes that grading is supposed to serve on every criterion:

1. *Uphold high academic standards.* It upholds high academic standards if we set the criteria for acceptable work above a C level. We grade work all-credit or no-credit, so the stakes for students are higher. These higher stakes coupled with higher standards motivate students to learn more and do higher quality work.

2. *Reflect student learning outcomes.* It yields grades that are directly tied to the students' actual learning and to their achievement, or lack thereof, of the learning outcomes of the course. At the same time, it shifts students' attention away from points and assignment grades to outcomes achievement. In addition, both specs grading and outcomes assessment are pass/fail propositions. In fact, course grades can in turn be tied to program outcomes, eliminating any extra program assessment steps.

3. *Motivate students to learn.* It motivates students to want to learn by emphasizing learning and outcomes achievement over grades per se, cultivating a learning over a performance orientation. In addition, it builds in multiple opportunities for student choice and control not only within and between assignments but also for the final grade itself.

4. *Motivate students to excel.* It motivates students to excel by both requiring high-quality products to earn credit and, as just stated, making students want to learn. Without partial credit, inferior work and minimal effort leads to failure.

5. *Discourage cheating.* It discourages cheating by reducing students' motivation and ability to cheat. It is more difficult to cheat on assessments that are authentic and that focus on higher-order cognitive skills and creativity. Moreover, students will find cheating less appealing when they want to learn and excel and can choose aspects of their assessments and their grades.

6. *Reduce student stress.* It reduces student stress by giving students more control over their academic success, a clearer picture of faculty expectations, more choice and volition, and a more accurate handle on what they can and cannot do at satisfactory levels. In addition, safety-net mechanisms such as tokens and the opportunity to revise or drop unacceptable work allow for flexibility and second chances.

7. *Make students feel responsible for their grades.* It fosters students' sense of responsibility for their grades by allowing them to choose how much and how deeply they will master the course material, knowing that their decisions will determine their grade. The possibility of instructor whim or taste affecting their grade is minimized. As long as they know what they have to do for each grade, they realize that the responsibility for earning a grade rests squarely on them.

8. *Minimize conflict between faculty and students.* For faculty, it minimizes conflict with students by requiring faculty to provide clear, detailed expectations for assignments and tests. On the other side, it increases students' sense of responsibility for their grades, thereby reducing grade-grubbing and grading protests. In addition, the safety-net mechanisms remove at least some uncomfortable interactions, such as requests for extensions and other special treatment. While specs grading permits extensions, it builds in automatic costs for them. Relatedly, by doing away with points, whether in part or entirely, it reduces or eliminates the likelihood of students pressuring faculty for more points, justified or not. It can also incorporate rewards for students to plan ahead and submit work on time or even early.

9. *Save faculty time.* It saves faculty time by simplifying the grading process. Preparing a one-level rubric with clear specs should require no more time than preparing a four- or five-level rubric—and may require even less. The grading process involves looking only for certain features in a student's work. A student product either meets the standard for acceptability or it doesn't. Instructors need not spend time making hair-splitting decisions about how much partial credit to allocate or writing detailed justifications for not giving full credit. In addition, students' complaints about their grades are less likely. As classes grow larger and teaching loads heavier, we have to find ways to save faculty time. Better that instructors focus more on student learning and less on grading.

10. *Give students feedback they will use.* It gives students feedback they will use because they can view the feedback as more than just the instructor's justification for subtracting points. Rather, they are more likely to take it as helpful, well-meaning, constructive advice on how to do better next time. In fact, faculty no longer have to justify taking off points and splitting hairs of quality. These factors change the power dynamics between faculty and students. With feedback and evaluation decoupled, the instructor's role shifts from an evaluative foe to a coach.

11. *Make expectations clear.* It makes expectations clear by having faculty focus their energy on developing detailed directions and requirements for all assessments and communicating them clearly to their students. This is the instructor's most time-consuming task, but it needs to be done for only one

level of performance—what is acceptable—and not for several levels, as a grading rubric requires.

12. *Foster higher-order cognitive development and creativity.* It fosters higher-order cognitive development and creativity by allowing faculty to grade student-constructed work more easily and quickly with a one-level rubric.

13. *Assess authentically.* It encourages authentic assessment in two ways: by making it easy and quicker for faculty to assess authentic, student-constructed products and by mimicking the way licensing exams and most other work is assessed in the real world.

14. *Have high interrater agreement.* It promotes high interrater agreement because its assessment standards delineate only two rating options, satisfactory or unsatisfactory. In addition, it emphasizes explicating clear criteria for a satisfactory performance. On both counts, it allows less room for disagreement.

15. *Be simple.* It is simple in several ways. The grading rubric for student-constructed work has only one level, and faculty need not make decisions about partial credit. Furthermore, the option of bundling assessments streamlines the grading structure and avoids the complexity of many different, independent assignments and tests.

As mentioned, realizing these benefits depends on how well and how completely a specs grading schema is implemented. Even with the best effort, no grading system will work perfectly in all classes at all times. Still, specs grading comes much closer than the current traditional grading system to achieving the objectives that learning incentives and sanctions are meant to meet. In fact, the current system yields few, if any, of the benefits listed here under the best of circumstances. More often than not, it gets in the way of student learning and undermines faculty morale. It is time to replace it with a more promising alternative. Specs grading provides a hospitable environment for learning.

REFERENCES

Achacoso, M. V. (2004). Post-test analysis: A tool for developing students' metacognitive awareness and self-regulation. In M. V. Achacoso & M. D. Svinivki (Eds.), *New directions for teaching and learning, No. 100: Alternative strategies for evaluating student learning* (pp. 115–119). San Francisco, CA: Jossey-Bass.

American College Health Association. (2013). *National college health assessment: Spring 2013 reference group executive summary.* Hanover, MD: Author. Available at http://www.acha-ncha.org/docs/ACHA-NCHA-II_ReferenceGroup_Executive Summary_Spring2013.pdf

American Institutes for Research. (2006). *The literacy of America's college students.* Washington, DC: Author.

Anderson, L. W., & Krathwohl, D. R. (2000). *A taxonomy for learning, teaching, and assessing: A revision of Bloom's Taxonomy of Educational Objectives.* Boston, MA: Allyn & Bacon.

Andrews, B. W. (2004). Musical contracts: Fostering student participation in the instructional process. *International Journal of Music Education, 22*(3), 219–229.

Arum, R., & Roksa, J. (2011). *Academically adrift: Limited learning on college campuses.* Chicago, IL: University of Chicago Press.

Atlas, J. L. (2007). The end of the course: Another perspective. *The Teaching Professor, 21*(6), 3.

Babcock, P., & Marks, M. (2011). The falling time cost of college: Evidence from half a century of time use data. *Review of Economics and Statistics, 93*(2), 468–478. Available at http://www.mitpressjournals.org/doi/pdf/10.1162/REST_a_00093

Bandura, A. (1977). *Social learning theory.* New York, NY: General Learning Press.

Bandura, A. (1997). *Self-efficacy: The exercise of control.* New York, NY: W. H. Freeman.

Barkley, E. F. (2009). *Student engagement techniques: A handbook for college faculty.* San Francisco, CA: Jossey-Bass.

Beare, P. G. (1986, October). The contract: An individualized approach to competency-based learning and evaluation. In *Proceedings of the 15th Annual Conference of the International Society for Individualized Instruction,* Atlanta, GA (ERIC Document Reproduction Service No. ED 276437). Available at http://files.eric.ed.gov/fulltext/ED276437.pdf

Beatty, I. (2012, February). *New ideas from physics education research that could change the way you envision your teaching and learning.* Concurrent session presented at Lilly South Conference on College Teaching, Greensboro, SC.

Benton, T. H. (2006, April 14). The 7 deadly sins of students. *The Chronicle of Higher Education.* Available at http://chronicle.com/article/The-7-Deadly-Sins-of-Students/46719/

Berrett, D. (2014a, March 19). In curricular clashes, completion can vie with quality. *The Chronicle of Higher Education.* Available at http://chronicle.com/article/In-Curricular-Clashes/145385/

Berrett, D. (2014b, March 11). Missouri budget tiff exposes doubts about competency-based education. *The Chronicle of Higher Education.* Available at http://chronicle.com/article/Missouri-Budget-Tiff-Exposes/145277/

Berry, P., Thornton, B., & Baker, R. (2006). Demographics of digital cheating: Who cheats, and what we can do about it. In M. Murray (Ed.), *Proceedings of the ninth annual conference of the Southern Association for Information Systems* (pp. 82–87). Jacksonville, FL: Jacksonville University, Davis College of Business.

Bloom, B. (1968). Learning for mastery. *Evaluation Comment, 1*(2), 1–12.

Bloom, B. (1971). Mastery learning. In J. H. Block (Ed.), *Mastery learning: Theory and practice* (pp. 47–63). New York, NY: Holt, Rinehart & Winston.

Bloom, B., & Associates. (1956). *Taxonomy of educational objectives.* New York, NY: David McKay.

Boak, G. (1998). *A complete guide to learning contracts.* Brookfield, VT: Gower.

Bowen, J. A. (2012). *Teaching naked: How moving technology out of your college classroom will improve student learning.* San Francisco, CA: Jossey-Bass.

Bransford, J. D., Brown, A. L., & Cocking, A. R. (2000). *How people learn: Brain, mind, experience, and school.* Washington, DC: National Research Council, National Academy Press.

Carlson, S. (2013, September 30). Competency-based education goes mainstream in Wisconsin. *The Chronicle of Higher Education.* Available at http://chronicle.com/article/Competency-Based-Education/141871/

Chan, S. W., & Wai-tong, C. (2000). Implementing contract learning in a clinical context: Report on a study. *Journal of Advanced Nursing, 31*(2), 298–305.

Chickering, A. W., & Gamson, Z. F. (1987). Seven principles for good practice in undergraduate education. *AAHE Bulletin, 39*(7) 3–7. Available at http://www.aahea.org/aahea/articles/sevenprinciples1987.htm

Chun, M. (2010). Taking teaching to (performance) task: Linking pedagogical and assessment practices. *Change, 42*(2), 22–29.

Chyung, S. Y. (2007). Invisible motivation of online adult learners during contract learning. *Journal of Educators Online, 4*(1). Available at http://www.thejeo.com/Volume4Number1/ChyungFinal.pdf

Codde, J. R. (2006). *Using learning contracts in the college classroom.* Available at http://www.msu.edu/user/coddejos/contract.htm

Cooper, M. M., & Sandi-Urena, S. (2009). Design and validation of an instrument to assess metacognitive skillfulness in chemistry problem solving. *Journal of Chemical Education, 86*(2), 240–245. Available at http://pubs.acs.org/doi/abs/10.1021/ed086p240

Costa, A. L., & Kallick, B. (2000). Getting into the habit of reflection. *Educational Leadership, 57*(7), 60–62.

Covey, S. R. (2013). *The 7 habits of highly effective people.* New York, NY: Rosetta Books.

Cuseo, J. (2007). The empirical case against large class size: Adverse effects on teaching, learning, and retention of first-year students. *Journal of Faculty Development, 21*(1), 5–21.

Dahlgren, L. O., Fejes, A., Abrandt-Dahlgren, M., & Trowald, N. (2009). Grading systems, features of assessment and students' approaches to learning. *Teaching in Higher Education, 14*(2), 185–194.

Davidson, C. (2009, July 26). How to crowdsource grading. [Web log post]. Available at http://www.hastac.org/blogs/cathy-davidson/how-crowdsource-grading

Deci, E. L., & Ryan, R. M. (1985). *Intrinsic motivation and self-determination in human behavior.* New York, NY: Plenum.

Delohery, P., & McLaughlin, G. (1971, September 27). Pass-fail grading. *O.I.R. Report, 4* (ERIC Document Reproduction Service No. ED O56651). Available at http://eric.ed.gov/?q=Pass-fail+grading&id=ED056651

Dobrow, S. R., Smith, W. K., & Posner, M. A. (2011). Managing the grading paradox: Leveraging the power of choice in the classroom. *Academy of Management Learning & Education, 10*(2), 261–276.

Dweck, C. S. (2007). *Mindset: The new psychology of success.* New York, NY: Random House.

Dweck, C. S., & Leggett, E. (1988). A social-cognitive approach to motivation and personality. *Psychological Review, 95,* 256–273.

Elbow, P. (2009). A unilateral grading contract to improve learning and teaching. *College Composition and Communication, 61*(2), 244–268. Available at http://works.bepress.com/peter_elbow/39

Elliott, E. S., & Dweck, C. S. (1988). Goals: An approach to motivation and achievement. *Journal of Personality and Social Psychology, 54,* 5–12.

Field, K. (2013, February 11). Colleges ask government to clarify rules for credit based on competency. *The Chronicle of Higher Education.* Available at http://chronicle.com/article/Colleges-Ask-Education-Dept/137225/

Fink, L. D. (2003). *Creating significant learning experiences: An integrated approach to designing college courses.* San Francisco, CA: Jossey-Bass.

Fischer, K. W., & Bidell, T. R. (1998). Dynamic development of psychological structures in action and thought. In R. M. Lerner (Ed.), *Handbook of child psychology. Vol 1: Theoretical models of human development* (5th ed., pp. 467–561). New York: Wiley.

Forrest, S. P., & Peterson, T. O. (2008). It's called andragogy. *Academy of Management Learning and Education, 5*(1), 113–122.

Fox, J. (2010). Establishing relevance. *The Teaching Professor, 24*(5), 1.

Fraser, J. A. H. (1990, November). *Student reaction to learning contracts.* Paper presented at the Conference of Atlantic Educators, Halifax, NS, Canada. (ERIC Document Reproduction Service No. ED 328196)

Fry, R. (2014, February 28). For Millennials, a bachelor's degree continues to pay off, but a master's earns even more. *FacTank: News in the Numbers.* Pew Research Center. Available at http://www.pewresearch.org/fact-tank/2014/02/28/for-millennials-a-bachelors-degree-continues-to-pay-off-but-a-masters-earns-even-more/

Gabriel, K. F. (2008). *Teaching unprepared students: Strategies for promoting success and retention in higher education.* Sterling, VA: Stylus.

Gatta, L. A. (1973). An analysis of the pass-fail grading system as compared to the conventional grading system in high school chemistry. *Journal of Research in Science Teaching, 10*(1), 3–12.

Gawande, A. (2009). *The checklist manifesto: How to get things right.* New York, NY: Metropolitan Books.

Glenn, D. (2010a, May 9). Carol Dweck's attitude: It's not about how smart you are. *The Chronicle of Higher Education.* Available at http://chronicle.com/article/Carol-Dwecks-Attitude/65405/

Glenn, D. (2010b, February 7). How students can improve by studying themselves: Researchers at CUNY's Graduate Center push "self-regulated learning." *The Chronicle of Higher Education.* Available at http://chronicle.com/article/Struggling-Students-Can-Imp/64004/

Gold, R. M., Reilly, A., Silberman, R., & Lehr, R. (1971). Academic achievement declines under pass-fail grading. *Journal of Experimental Education, 39*(3), 17–21.

Hammons, J. O., & Barnsley, J. R. (1992). Everything you need to know about developing a grading plan for your course (well, almost). *Journal on Excellence in College Teaching, 3,* 51–68.

Hart Research Associates. (2010). *Raising the bar: Employers' views on college learning in the wake of the economic downturn.* Washington, DC: Author.

Hazard, L. L. (2011). *Time management, motivation, and procrastination: Understanding and teaching students self-regulatory behaviors.* Innovative Educators webinar broadcast live and recorded November 4.

Henfiled, V., & Waldron, H. (1988). The use of competency statements to facilitate individualized learning. *Nursing Education, 8,* 205–211.

Hiller, T. B., & Hietapelto, A. B. (2001). Contract grading: Encouraging commitment to the learning process through voice in the evaluation process. *Journal of Management Education, 25*(6), 660–684.

Hutton, P. A. (2006). Understanding student cheating and what educators can do about it. *College Teaching, 54*(1), 171–176.

Jaschik, S. (2009, August 3). Getting out of grading. *Inside Higher Ed.* Available at http://www.insidehighered.com/news/2009/08/03/grading

Johnson, V. E. (2003). *Grade inflation: A crisis in college education.* New York, NY: Springer-Verlag.

Kalman, C. S. (2007). *Successful science and engineering teaching in colleges and universities.* Bolton, MA: Anker.

Karlins, M., Kaplan, M., & Stuart, W. (1969). Academic attitudes and performance as a function of differential grading systems: An evaluation of Princeton's pass-fail system. *Journal of Experimental Education, 37*(3), 38–50. Available at http://www.jstor.org/stable/20157034

Kazin, C. (2012, December). *College for America at Southern New Hampshire University.* Presentation at the annual meeting of the New England Association of Schools and Colleges, Boston, MA.

Kellogg, A. (2002, February 15). Students plagiarize online less than many think, a new study finds. *The Chronicle of Higher Education.* Available at http://chronicle. com/article/Students-Plagiarize-Online-/24131/

Kennedy, M. (2012, December). *The Liberal Education Program, Southern Connecticut State University.* Presentation at the annual meeting of the New England Association of Schools and Colleges, Boston, MA.

Kirkman, S., Coughlin, K., & Kromrey, J. (2007). Correlates of satisfaction and success in self-directed learning: Relationships with school experience, course format, and Internet use. *International Journal of Self-Directed Learning, 4*(1), 39–50.

Kitchener, K. S., & King, P. M. (1985/1996). *Reflective judgment scoring manual with examples.* Unpublished manuscript, Bowling Green State University and the University of Denver.

Kleiner, C., & Lord, M. (1999, November 22). The cheating game. *U.S. News & World Report, 127*(20), 55–66.

Knowles, M. S. (1975). *Self-directed learning: A guide for learners and teachers.* Chicago, IL: Follett.

Knowles, M. (1980). *The modern practice of adult education: From pedagogy to andragogy.* Englewood Cliffs, NJ: Prentice-Hall.

Knowles, M. S. (1984). *The adult learner: A neglected species* (3rd ed.). Houston, TX: Gulf Publishing.

Knowles, M. S. (1986). *Using learning contracts: Practical approaches to individualizing and structuring learning.* San Francisco, CA: Jossey-Bass.

Kuhn, T. S. (1996). *The structure of scientific revolutions* (3rd ed.). Chicago, IL: University of Chicago Press.

Kulik, C., Kulik, J., & Bangert-Drowns, R. (1990). Effectiveness of mastery learning programs: A meta-analysis. *Review of Educational Research, 60*(2), 265–306.

Kunkel, S. W. (2002). Consultant learning: A model for student-directed learning in management education. *Journal of Management Education, 26*(2), 121–138.

LeBlanc, P. J. (2013, January 31). Accreditation in a rapidly changing world. *Inside Higher Ed.* Available at http://www.insidehighered.com/views/2013/01/31/ competency-based-education-and-regional-accreditation

Leff, L. L. (n.d.). *Contract grading in teaching computer programming.* Available at http://faculty.wiu.edu/D-Leff/GRADCONT.HTM

Levine, A., & Dean, D. R. (2012). *Generation on a tightrope: A portrait of today's college students* (3rd ed.). San Francisco, CA: Jossey-Bass.

Lloyd, D. A. (1992). Commentary: Pass-fail grading fails to meet the grade. *Academic Medicine, 67*(9), 583–584.

Locke, E. A., & Latham. G. P. (1990). *A theory of goal setting and task performance.* Upper Saddle River, NJ: Prentice Hall.

Mangan, K. (2013, November 18). Some community colleges pioneer competency-based credentials. *The Chronicle of Higher Education.* Available at http://chronicle.com/article/Some-Community-Colleges/143151/

Mānoa Writing Program. (n.d.). *Writing Matters #5: Helping students make connections: A self-assessment approach.* University of Hawaii at Mānoa. Available at http://manoa.hawaii.edu/mwp/program-research/writing-matters/wm-5

Musca, T. (Producer), & Menéndez, R. (Director). (1988). *Stand and deliver* [Motion pictrue]. USA: Warner Bros.

Nathan, R. (2005). *My freshman year: What a professor learned by becoming a student.* Ithaca, NY: Cornell University Press.

National Survey of Student Engagement. (2013). *A fresh look at student engagement: Annual results 2013.* Bloomington, IN: Indiana University Center for Postsecondary Research. Available at http://nsse.iub.edu/NSSE_2013_Results/pdf/NSSE_2013_Annual_Results.pdf

Nicol, D. J., & Macfarlane-Dick, D. (2006). Formative assessment and self-regulated learning: A model and seven principles of good feedback practice. *Studies in Higher Education, 32*(2), 199–218.

Nilson, L. B. (2007). *The graphic syllabus and the outcomes map: Communicating your course.* San Francisco, CA: Jossey-Bass.

Nilson, L. B. (2009). Editor's introduction: The educational developer as magician. In L. B. Nilson & J. E. Miller (Eds.), *To improve the academy: Vol. 27. Resources for faculty, instructional, and organizational development* (pp. 3–13). San Francisco, CA: Jossey-Bass.

Nilson, L. B. (2010). *Teaching at its best: A research-based resource for college instructors* (3rd ed.). San Francisco, CA: Jossey-Bass.

Nilson, L. B. (2012). Time to raise questions about student ratings. In J. E. Groccia & L. Cruz (Eds.), *To improve the academy: Vol. 31. Resources for faculty, instructional, and organizational development* (pp. 213–228). San Francisco, CA: Jossey-Bass.

Nilson, L. B. (2013). *Creating self-regulated learners: Strategies to strengthen students' self-awareness and learning skills.* Sterling, VA: Stylus.

Nuhfer, E. D., & Knipp, D. (2003). The knowledge survey: A tool for all reasons. In C. Wehlburg & S. Chadwick-Blossey (Eds.), *To improve the academy: Vol. 21. Resources for faculty, instructional, and organizational development* (pp. 59–78). Boston, MA: Anker.

Ottenhoff, J. (2011). Learning how to learn: Metacognition in liberal education. *Liberal Education, 97*(3/4). Available at http://www.aacu.org/liberaleducation/le-sufa11/ottenhoff.cfm?utm_source=pubs&utm_medium=blast&utm_campaign=libedsufa2011

Perkins, D. (2008, November). *Learning portfolios and metacognition.* Session presented at the National Association of Geoscience Teachers (NAGT) Workshops: The Role of Metacognition in Teaching Geoscience, Carleton College, Northfield, MN. Available at http://serc.carleton.edu/NAGTWorkshops/metacognition/perkins.html

Perry, D. M. (2014, March 17). Faculty members are not cashiers: Why the "customer service" lingo is bad for students. *The Chronicle of Higher Education.* Available at https://chronicle.com/article/Faculty-Members-Are-Not/145363/

Perry, W. G. (1968). *Forms of intellectual and ethical development in the college years: A scheme.* New York, NY: Holt, Rinehart & Winston.

Polczynski, J. J., & Shirland, L. E. (1977). Expectancy theory and contract grading combined as an effective motivational force for college students. *Journal of Educational Research, 70*(5), 238–241.

Redmond, B. F., & Perrin, J. J. (2014). *Goal setting theory.* PSYCH 484: Work Attitudes and Job Motivation, Pennsylvania State University. Available at https://wikispaces.psu.edu/display/PSYCH484/6.+Goal+Setting+Theory

Rhem, J. (2011). Laura Gibbs: Online course lady. *National Teaching & Learning Forum, 21*(1), 1–5.

Ripley, A. (2013). *The smartest kids in the world and how they got that way.* New York, NY: Simon & Schuster.

Robbins, T. L., & Kegley, K. (2010). Playing with Thinkertoys to build creative abilities through online instruction. *Thinking Skills and Creativity, 5*(1), 40–48. Available at http://www.sciencedirect.com/science?_ob=ArticleListURL&_method=list&_ArticleListID=-603689322&_sort=r&_st=13&view=c&md5=de52dc1e344dcabaa75bd3db84a20cab&searchtype=a

Robins, L. S., Fantone, J. C., Oh, M. S., Alexander, G. L., Shlafer, M., & Davis, W. K. (1995). The effect of pass/fail grading and weekly quizzes on first-year students' performances and satisfaction. *Academic Medicine, 70*(4), 327–329.

Rohe, D. E., Barrier, P. A., & Clark, M. M. (2006). The benefits of pass-fail grading on stress, mood, and group cohesion in medical school. Available at http://eds.a.ebscohost.com/ehost/pdfviewer/pdfviewer?sid=d327ba88-bbb2-43ea-94c5-503a98fbcef5%40sessionmgr4005&vid=2&hid=4203

Rojstaczer, S., & Healy, C. (2012). Where A is ordinary: The evolution of American college and university grading, 1940–2009. *Teachers College Record, 114*(7), 1–23. Available at http://www.tcrecord.org/content.asp?contentid=16473

Sabin, B. M. (n.d.). Using learning contracts in the community college. Unpublished manuscript available at http://www.brucesabin.com/pdf_files/learning_contracts.pdf

Samson, G. E., Graue, M. E., Weinstein, T., & Walberg, H. J. (1984). Academic and occupational performance: A quantitative synthesis. *American Educational Research Journal, 21*(2), 311–321.

Schneider, J., & Hutt, E. (2013). Making the grade: A history of the A–F marking scheme. Unpublished manuscript available at http://academics.holycross.edu/files/Education/schneider/Making_the_Grade_JCS_pre-pub.pdf

Schraw, G., & Dennison, R. S. (1994). Assessing metacognitive awareness. *Contemporary Educational Psychology, 19*, 460–475. Available through http://scholar.google.com

The Self-Regulated Learning Program. (n.d.). Available at http://www.selfregulatedlearning.blogspot.com/

Singleton-Jackson, J. A., Jackson, D. L., & Reinhardt, J. (2010). Students as consumers of knowledge: Are they buying what we're selling? *Innovative Higher Education, 35*(4), 343–358.

Stallings, W. M., & Smock, H. R. (1971). The pass-fail grading option at a state university: A five semester evaluation. *Journal of Educational Measurement, 8*(3), 153–160. Available at http://www.jstor.org/stable/1434384

Stevens, D. D., & Cooper, J. C. (2009). *Journal keeping: How to use reflective writing for effective learning, teaching, professional insight, and positive change.* Sterling, VA: Stylus.

Stevens, D. D., & Levi, A. J. (2012). *Introduction to rubrics: An assessment tool to save grading time, convey effective feedback, and promote student learning* (2nd ed.). Sterling, VA: Stylus.

Strawbridge, G. (1999). The effectiveness of andragogical instruction as compared with traditional instruction in philosophy courses. *PAACE Journal of Lifelong Learning, 8,* 41–52.

Suskie, L. (2004). *Assessing student learning: A common sense guide.* San Francisco, CA: Jossey-Bass.

Svinicki, M. (2004). *Learning and motivation in postsecondary classrooms.* San Francisco, CA: Jossey-Bass.

Tinto, V. (n.d.). *Taking student success seriously: Rethinking the first year of college.* Available at http://www.purdue.edu/foundationsofexcellence/documents/FOE%20 Documents/Taking%20Success%20Seriously.pdf. Original version published in 1999, *NACADA Journal, 19*(2), 5–9.

Towson University. (2006). *Faculty handbook.* Towson, MD: Author.

Vander Schee, B. (2009, September). Increasing motivation in Capstone: Strategic Management: An alternative grading approach. Paper presented at the Marketing Management Association Fall Educators' Annual Conference, St. Louis, MO.

Venditti, P. (2010, June 10). Re: End of Semester Sanity Strategies? Message posted to the POD Network electronic mailing list, archived at https://listserv.nd.edu/ cgi-bin/wa?A2=ind1006&L=POD&T=0&F=&S=&P=67803

von Wittich, B. (1972). The impact of the pass-fail system upon achievement of college students. *Journal of Higher Education, 43*(6), 499–508. Available at http:// www.jstor.org/stable/1978896?seq=1

Vosti, K. L., & Jacobs, C. D. (1999). Outcome measurement in postgraduate year one of graduates from a medical school with a pass/fail grading. *Academic Medicine, 74*(5), 547–549.

Waldenberger, S. (2012). *Technology and human values.* Syllabus for HUM 205. Yavapai Community College. Available at http://ychumanities.net/ ychum205/2012/08/14/welcome-to-hum-205/

Walvoord, B. E., & Anderson, V. J. (2009). *Effective grading: A tool for learning and assessment in college* (2nd ed.). San Francisco, CA: Jossey-Bass.

Warrington, A. C., Hietapelto, A. B., & Joyce, W. B. (2003, August). *Contract grading: Impact on student learning and motivation in accounting and management classes.* Poster session presented at the annual meeting of the American Accounting Association, Honolulu, HI.

Weimer, M. (2002). *Learner-centered teaching: Five key changes to practice.* San Francisco, CA: Jossey-Bass.

Wigfield, A., & Eccles, J. (2000). Expectancy-value theory of achievement motivation. *Contemporary Educational Psychology, 25*, 68–81.

Wiggins, G., & McTighe, J. (2005). *Understanding by design* (2nd ed.). Alexandria, VA: Association for Supervision and Curriculum Development.

Wirth, K. R. (2008, November). *A metacurriculum on metacognition.* Opening keynote address presented at the National Association of Geoscience Teachers (NAGT) Workshops: The Role of Metacognition in Teaching Geoscience, Carleton College, Northfield, MN. Available at http://serc.carleton.edu/NAGTWorkshops/metacognition/wirth.html

Wirth, K. R., & Perkins, D. (2008). *Learning to learn.* Available at http://www.macalester.edu/geology/wirth/learning.pdf

Wolcott, S. K. (2006, February 9). *Steps for better thinking.* Available at http://www.wolcottlynch.com/EducatorResources.html

Wolcott, S. K., & Lynch, C. L. (2006a, January 26). *Steps for better thinking performance patterns.* Available at http://www.wolcottlynch.com/EducatorResources.html

Wolcott, S. K., & Lynch, C. L. (2006b, February 9). *Templates for designing assignment questions.* Available at http://www.wolcottlynch.com/Downloadable_Files/Assignment%20Templates_060209.pdf

Young, J. R. (2011, August 7). Professors cede grading power to outsiders—even computers. *The Chronicle of Higher Education.* Available at http://chronicle.com/article/To-Justify-Every-A-Some/128528/

Zander, R. S., & Zander, B. (2000). *The art of possibility: Transforming professional and personal life.* Cambridge, MA: Harvard University Business Press.

Zimmerman, B. J., Moylan, A., Hudesman, J., White, N., & Flugman, B. (2011). Enhancing self-reflection and mathematics achievement of at-risk urban technical college students. *Psychological Test and Assessment Modeling, 53*(1), 141–160. Available at http://p16277.typo3server.info/fileadmin/download/ptam/1-2011_20110328/07_Zimmermann.pdf

ABOUT THE AUTHOR

Linda B. Nilson is founding director of the Office of Teaching Effectiveness and Innovation (OTEI) at Clemson University and author of *Teaching at Its Best: A Research-Based Resource for College Instructors*, now in its third edition (Jossey-Bass, 2010; fourth edition in planning stages); *The Graphic Syllabus and the Outcomes Map: Communicating Your Course* (Jossey-Bass, 2007); and *Creating Self-Regulated Learners: Strategies to Strengthen Students' Self-Awareness and Learning Skills* (Stylus, 2013). She also coedited *Enhancing Learning With Laptops in the Classroom* (Jossey-Bass, 2005) and Volumes 25 through 28 of *To Improve the Academy: Resources for Faculty, Instructional, and Organizational Development* (Anker, 2007, 2008; Jossey-Bass, 2009, 2010). *To Improve the Academy* is the major publication of the Professional and Organizational Development (POD) Network in Higher Education.

Dr. Nilson's career as a full-time faculty development director spans 25 years. In this time, she has published many articles and book chapters and has given more than 500 keynotes and workshops at conferences, colleges, and universities both nationally and internationally. She has also conducted dozens of webinars for Wiley and Magna Publications. She has spoken on numerous topics related to course design, best teaching and assessment practices, scholarly productivity, and academic career matters. In her recent articles, she documents the instability of faculty development careers, raises serious questions about the validity of student ratings, and describes instructor-friendly ways to measure course-level learning that are suitable for the most rigorous faculty review.

Before coming to Clemson University, Dr. Nilson directed the teaching centers at Vanderbilt University and the University of California, Riverside, where she developed the disciplinary cluster approach to training teaching assistants out of a centralized unit. She has also taught graduate seminars on college teaching. She entered the area of educational/faculty development while she was a member of the sociology faculty at UCLA. After distinguishing herself as an excellent instructor, her department selected her to set up and supervise its teaching assistant training program. In sociology, her research focused on occupations and work, social stratification, political sociology, and disaster behavior.

Dr. Nilson has held leadership positions in the POD Network, Toastmasters International, Mensa, and the Southern Regional Faculty and Instructional Development Consortium. She was a National Science Foundation fellow at the University of Wisconsin, Madison, where she received her master's and doctoral degrees in sociology. She completed her undergraduate work in three years at the University of California, Berkeley, where she was elected to Phi Beta Kappa.

Dr. Nilson lives with her retired husband, Greg, and their somewhat pampered miniature schnauzer in Anderson, South Carolina.

INDEX

Linda Nilson provides the theoretical background to student self-regulation, the evidence that it enhances achievement, and the strategies to help students develop it. She presents an array of tested activities and assignments through which students can progressively reflect on, monitor, and improve their learning skills; describes how they can be integrated with different course components and on various schedules; and elucidates how to intentionally and seamlessly incorporate them into course design to effectively meet disciplinary and student development objectives. Recognizing that most faculty are unfamiliar with these strategies, she also recommends how to prepare for introducing them into the classroom and adding more as instructors become more confident using them.

The book concludes with descriptions of courses from different fields to offer models and ideas for implementation.

Sty/us

22883 Quicksilver Drive
Sterling, VA 20166-2102

Subscribe to our e-mail alerts: www.Styluspub.com

Also by Linda B. Nilson

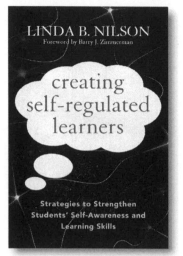

Creating Self-Regulated Learners
Strategies to Strengthen Students' Self-Awareness and Learning Skills
Foreword by Barry J. Zimmerman

"Linda Nilson has done it again! Her newest book on self-regulated learning should be on every faculty member's shelf, but more importantly, it should be in every student's hands. It would not be an exaggeration to say that I owe, in part, my lucky selection as a Carnegie Foundation/ CASE U.S. Professor of the Year to reading and applying many of the teaching and learning principles that she has formulated and refined for years and that she now outlines in *Creating Self-Regulated Learners*. The book is not only well researched, theoretical, and analytical, but also full of detailed, practical tips and resources. The focus is not on producing a bunch of magicians' tricks to bolster study skills; rather, Nilson stresses the importance of rethinking and redesigning our teaching and our courses to help students learn how to learn, giving them self-directed, self-assessing habits that transform them into reflective, life-long learners. Nilson's contributions to higher education are substantial, and this book is another gift to all of us who care about good teaching and helping students become autonomous, deep learners."

—**John Zubizarreta**, *Professor of English, Director of Honors and Faculty Development, Columbia College; Past President, National Collegiate Honors Council; and Carnegie Foundation/CASE U.S. Professor of the Year*

"Linda Nilson has provided a veritable gold mine of effective learning strategies that are easy for faculty to teach and for students to learn. Most students can turn poor course performance into success if they are taught even a few of the strategies presented. However, relatively few students will implement new strategies if they are not required to do so by instructors. Nilson shows how to seamlessly introduce learning strategies into classes, thereby maximizing the possibility that students will become self-regulated learners who take responsibility for their own learning."

—**Saundra McGuire**, *Assistant Vice Chancellor (Ret.) and Professor of Chemistry, Louisiana State University*

Most of our students neither know how learning works nor what they have to do to ensure it, to the detriment both of their studies and their development as lifelong learners.

The point of departure for this book is the literature on self-regulated learning that tells us that deep, lasting, independent learning requires learners to bring into play a range of cognitive skills, affective attitudes, and even physical activities; and that self-regulation, which has little to do with measured intelligence, can be developed by just about anyone and is a fundamental prerequisite of academic success.